Routledge Revivals

Economic Prospects – East and West

First published in 1987, this is an analysis of the contemporary breakdown of political and economic systems within the Eastern European communist countries. Rather than passively following the developments of this crisis, the author seeks instead to identify the reasons for failure and to examine alternative policies that offer solutions to these problems.

Jan Winiecki's work offers a comparative study of the Soviet-type economies of the East with the market economies of the West; providing a cause and effect analysis of each model, with possible scenarios for their future prospects.

T0361994

Economic Prospects - East and West

A view from the East

Jan Winiecki

Routledge
Taylor & Francis Group

First published in 1987
By The Centre for Research into Communist Economies

This edition first published in 2012 by Routledge
2 Park Square, Milton Park, Abingdon, Oxon, OX14 4RN

Simultaneously published in the USA and Canada
by Routledge
711 Third Avenue, New York, NY 10017

Routledge is an imprint of the Taylor & Francis Group, an informa business

Publisher's Note
The publisher has gone to great lengths to ensure the quality of this reprint but
points out that some imperfections in the original copies may be apparent.

Disclaimer
The publisher has made every effort to trace copyright holders and welcomes
correspondence from those they have been unable to contact.

ISBN 13: 978-0-415-69992-1 (hbk)
ISBN 13: 978-0-203-12267-9 (ebk)
ISBN 13: 978-0-415-51999-1 (pbk)

Economic Prospects-East and West

A view from the East

Jan Winiecki

Comment

Roger Clarke

Published by
THE CENTRE FOR RESEARCH INTO
COMMUNIST ECONOMIES
1987

Economic Prospects-
East and West

First published in May 1987
by
The Centre for Research into Communist Economies
c/o 2 Lord North Street, London SW1P 3LB

ISBN 0 948027 06 1

Printed in Great Britain by
Pika Print Limited, Genotin Road, Enfield, Middx. EN1 2AA

Contents

Foreword

When sending to the printers the first text by a Polish contributor, we wish to remember our colleague and friend, Janusz Zielinski. He came to Britain in 1968 after having been dismissed from the Warsaw Central School of Planning and Statistics. Most of his time in this country, he worked at the Institute of Soviet and East European Studies, University of Glasgow. His life was not easy because he had contracted a tropical disease while teaching in Africa, but his spirits were revived and he was full of hope for the future again when he became a British citizen and when it seemed that he would be able to visit his native country regularly. Janusz Zielinski expected that Polish experts and Polish authorities would be willing to listen to his scholarly findings and suggestions. However, what happened was a disaster — Zielinski was ordered to leave his homeland within twenty four hours and people associating with him had difficulties with the authorities. For Janusz this was a humiliation he could not forget and which disturbed him so much that he finally took his own life in 1979.

It is a great pity that, in the supposedly enlightened twentieth century, men are not prepared to listen to each other and to argue instead of laying down the law. Many impasses could have been avoided, had their perpetrators been willing to discuss them properly. We sincerely hope that things are changing — partly because of dire economic urgency — and that arguments will be, in the future, replied to by arguments rather than by prohibitions, expulsions and punishment.

At any rate, attempts at intimidation and insulation do not work and even less decisions taken under such circumstances, witness the text by Jan Winiecki. Our present author has spent his life behind what was called the Iron Curtain while it was still firmly in place. Nonetheless, he does not seem to lack either information or ideas to formulate his own clear views on matters economic East and West. On the contrary, his East-European experience appears to add a dimension to what an economist born and bred in the West could have said on the subject.

Jan Winiecki has also been exposed to the ire of the powers that be, although at a time when wiser councils would seem to have prevailed and people of different views are no longer pursued with quite the previous ferocity. We welcome this promise because

5

we believe that it is the only way to exchange views and find solutions for the present impasse.

The Constitution of the CRCE requires that its Trustees and Advisers dissociate themselves from the analysis contained in its publications, but we all hope that the text by Jan Winiecki from Warsaw with comments by Roger Clarke from Glasgow will attract a wide readership and that readers will learn from them and respond to them with scholarly arguments.

Ljubo Sirc

Economic Prospects-
East and West

A view from the East

Jan Winiecki

Biographical note

Dr. Jan Winiecki was born on 21 June 1938, in Sopot, in Poland. He studied economics at the Central School of Planning and Statistics at Warsaw University. He obtained his Doctorate in Economics in 1971. From 1971 to 1973 he was Head of the Division of Economic Studies, Centre for Scientific, Technical and Economic Information, Warsaw. From 1973 to the present he has been Associate Professor at a number of Research Institutes in Warsaw: until 1982 at the Department of International Economics at the Institute of International Affairs attatched to the Ministry of Foreign Affairs; in 1983 and 1984 at the Institute of Management at the Polish Academy of Sciences (from which he was forced to resign for political reasons); and since 1985 at the Institute of Labour Research.

From 1977-85 he was also Executive Secretary of the committee dealing with international economic problems in the "Poland 2000" futureological project of the Polish Academy of Sciences.

Dr. Winiecki has written a number of books including *"Prospects for International Business"*, Pism Publishers, Warsaw, 1983, and *"The Distorted World of Soviet-type Economies"*, Croom Helm, forthcoming. He has also published extensively in Polish and, more recently, in Western, scholarly journals on the subjects of centrally planned economies and international trade. He is also the editor of *"Perspectives for the World Economy"* published by the "Poland 2000" project in 1983 in Warsaw in English.

Dr. Winiecki is married and has one grown-up child. He lives in Warsaw.

Acknowledgment

The CRCE wishes to thank the Editors of *Soviet Studies* for permission to reprint parts of Jan Winiecki's papers published in July and October 1986. For reasons of simplicity the original editorial style was retained and the CRCE is grateful to Roger Clarke for his willingness correspondingly to edit the sections not previously published.

Preface

The two essays included in this publication forecast highly dissimilar futures for the two areas — and systems — considered. In my view Soviet-type economies (the equivalent of "East" in the title) have entered an era of long-term decline. The decline looks irreversible under the existing model of central planning, whether modified or not.

At the same time, some political forces remain strongly opposed to the transformation of the economic subsystem into a market economy even if not entailing a change of the political subsystem. In other words, if the introduction of the market system were accompanied by a shift from totalitarianism to an "ordinary" autocratic regime rather than to a democratic one. Until those pillars of the Soviet system that benefit most from central planning withdraw their opposition, are forced to withdraw it, or are forced out of power, things will go from bad to worse. Moreover, as evidenced by the rapidly worsening environment and public health problems, the deterioration will not be confined to the economy.

In all probability then things will get worse, maybe much worse, before they get better. And since I do not expect such fundamental economic change to come about earlier than in the next five to ten years, I can see only one road from my vantage point — the road downhill.

Both essays are presented here in the same format. First, trends are analyzed, next current constraints upon and opportunities for future options are assessed, and finally scenarios are outlined. However, the same format is filled in with distinctly different contents for East and West.

In this author's view, the market system is comparable with the wheel in both its simplicity and its indispensability. The main problem of Soviet-type economies (STEs for short) is that their political subsystem has produced an economic subsystem that has been trying for decades on end — at great expense, effort, and sacrifice — to substitute the square for the wheel. All modifications that have ever taken place in STEs amounted by and large to smoothing the edges of the squares to make the movement less bumpy, while maintaining in all (real or pretended) seriousness that wagons run further on squares than on wheels.

Consequently, STEs — if they are to move forward at all — will have to tackle the fundamental task of "reinventing" the wheel. Mature market economies (the equivalent of the "West" in the title) have a much easier task. The wheel is disfigured somewhat, cracks have appeared here and there on its surface, it creaks at every second turn but it is unmistakeably the wheel. Since both the wheel and the knowledge how to repair it are available in the West, different scenarios tie economic prospects to the political will to repair the wheel and bear the repair costs.

When things get bad enough, people do even obvious and sensible things — according to George Shultz (quoted also elsewhere in the publication). It appears to me that by 1980-1982 things got bad enough in terms of the market system's ability to create wealth, for the willingness to repair the wheel to resurface — slowly and haltingly to reverse the collectivist and etatist trends that had impaired the market.

I then recognized — as did many others — that it was not just the change in political climate that supported the about-turn. Simplifying a little, both technological change and shifts in the unemployment structure have changed, in the last 10-to-15 years, from being impediments to being supporters of the market sytem (and, ultimately, a more liberal political order).

This is most important. A market-oriented political climate may peak or even recede (stirrings of destructive unreason are noticeable in the United States and France at the time of writing) but the changes imposed by technological and economic realities would appear to be strong enough to stop the ebb and even to expand the boundaries of market determined allocation of goods and serivces. Also, they will slowly affect the political balance in Western societies in favour of liberal and market-oriented parties of the so-called centre right.

Contrary to the scenarios for STEs, where all trends adversely affect the performance of the unreformable economic subsystem, the scenarios for Western market economies (MEs for short) look much more optimistic. Two out of three are predicated upon the continued reversal of collectivist and etatist trends that have impaired the market system's ability to create wealth and differ only in the degree of speed with which the reversal, or more precisely the change towards the new individualism, will continue.

The underlying forces of reversal make this outcome a most probable future but not the only possible one. The continued support of electoral majorities for the collectivist and etatist alternative to the liberal and market-oriented order may generate a scenario of economic decline not dissimilar from those outlined in the first part for STEs (except that the starting level of well-being would be much higher). Though I included such a scenario in the essay dealing with the West's futures, I regard it — fortunately — as not very likely to happen in the West as a whole and not much more probable even in some Western MEs.

The dissimilarity of East's and West's futures, as outlined in this publication, is striking. The West's prospects are infinitely better in terms of its ability to solve present problems and make the Western world wealthier and the life there more satisfying. Only the one scenario concerning a possible decline under the impact of continuing collectivist-etatist trends says otherwise and this scenario was given a very low-to-low probability. In contrast, the East's prospects as shown by most scenarios, are a continuing decline and, what is more, the scenarios envisaging a change of the economic subsystem have a very low probability, as least in the next 5-to-10 years.

The implications of such comparative perspective in practice are not to be underestimated. Since the distance between East and West will be increasing at an accelerated rate in the foreseeable future, economic competition — or whatever has been left of it since Khrushchev promised to "bury" capitalism — will soon be decided in the West's favour. Ideologically, the failure of the collectivist-etatist centralized solution will become obvious even to the most fervent believers in the Third World (the last place where such believers may still exist in significant numbers). Strategically, the East's decline will limit its ability to support economically its collectivist-etatist 'look-alikes' in the Third World. And even militarily, a weakened economic base will restrain the ability of the Soviet Union and its dependencies to raise both the military and non-military expenditures simultaneously. If the West does not make the fatal mistake of disarming itself both spiritually and militarily under the pressure from naive and impatient segments of its own societies, the balance of power — economic, ideological, and political — will decisively tilt in its favour, which in itself will make the world safer for democracy and prosperity, in the longer run inseparable from one another.

***

In conclusion, I wish to make three types of acknowledgements. My warmest thanks go to my colleagues in Poland and abroad with whom I so often discussed various issues and aspects of these essays. Writing down all the names would make my acknowledgements look like a phone directory.

Next my thanks go to the editors of *Soviet Studies* who kindly gave their permission to reprint my two articles published in Nos. 3 and 4 of 1986. Though revised and expanded, they are the core of the essay on the East's trends and prospects.

At the end, I would like to record a very special kind of gratitude. I wrote the drafts for the essays appearing here in the autumn of 1984. By then I had already been served the notice of dismissal from the Polish Academy of Sciences for my "politically unacceptable" professional views. Probably to prevent the further spreading of these "dangerous" liberal and market-oriented ideas I had also been barred from participating in my institute's activities. Since this decision also freed me from all those bureaucratic and pseudo-scholarly activities typical of academic institutions in the Soviet system, the period till the end of my employment contract turned into a highly desirable fellowship of sorts: I could devote most of my time to writing which enabled me *inter alia* to produce these essays. For this service, however inadvertently rendered, I do wish to thank the ideological policemen in the Academy of Sciences, from its secretary general to the director of the Institute of Management where I worked at the time.

The Author

Part I
The East

I.1. INTRODUCTORY REMARKS

The recent economic slowdown in Eastern Europe, coupled with the problems of indebtedness and balance of payments difficulties and falling living standards and open inflation, have generated many predictions that the centrally planned economies are entering an era of decline. The various interpretations presented in the West, and the few cautious and often oblique warnings published in the East have, however, offered very different answers to the question why this 'time of troubles' — to give Tonybee's term a somewhat different meaning — should differ from previous ones. Soviet-type economies have recovered from periods of difficulty in the past, to continue on their joyless course of growth without much prosperity. Sceptics have pointed out that most of the arguments put forward on this occasion have been advanced before.

The slowdown in the expansion of the labour supply is certainly familiar as a barrier to continuation of the type of growth seen in earlier periods. Nor are barriers to investment expansion new to analysts of Soviet-type economies. (STEs) The rigidity of the hierarchical system of management has also been cited as a cause of slow adjustment to economic change domestically (to say nothing of the world market), as has the inhibiting effect of risk aversion on technical change (in fact, on any change in routine). The list could easily be extended without adding much that is new, except the radical change in the relative price of energy. Some analysts have then looked at the cumulative effects, while others have added a socio-psychological and political dimension (in direct or indirect reference to the eruption in Poland that gave birth to the 'Solidarity' movement).

Without understating the significance of the economic and/or non-economic reasons usually put forward to explain the decline of the STEs, I find it rather difficult to accept that they provide a coherent explanation why the signs of decline have appeared in this particular period and why they can be expected to continue and intensify in the future, thus indicating a secular trend rather than the trough of another economic (and political) cycle. While basically in agreement with those stressing the prospects of long

15

term decline, I see the problem somewhat differently. In the subsequent discussion I outline what I regard as the most important causes of decline, some of them common to all analysts, some reinterpreted or new, and link particular causes to particular effects. I also distinguish the traditional causes of weak performance from those that have exerted an increasing effect recently, attempt to explain why the latter have become important now, and suggest what their future influence will be. Almost all the causes are endogenous to the system; problems in the world economy have only accelerated the onset of the 'time of troubles' in Soviet-type economies.

I.2 CAUSES – SYMPTOMS – EFFECTS

ENDOGENOUS CAUSES

A problem which arises in analysis of the performance of STEs is mistaking the symptoms for the causes. To give an example, the high resource intensity of these economies has often been cited as one of the causes of decline in the era of more costly resources. In reality, it is a set of long-standing factors specific to the system that results in an abnormally high level of resource use. High resource intensity is thus a symptom, not a cause. At the same time it is important to explain why the symptoms which these causes produce have become more serious of late.

DISTORTED MOTIVATION

We begin with a number of causes whose significance has increased recently:

(1) Analysts have long been pointing to the distorted motivations and the lack of the usual constraints on the behaviour of enterprises. As I have explained elsewhere (Winiecki, 1982), incentives at the enterprise level, for managers and workers alike, have always been positively correlated with the volume or value of output in a STE, but not, at the same time, negatively correlated with the costs of material inputs and factors of production. In consequence, enterprises have been encouraged to expand production at any cost, continuously increasing their demand for material inputs, using them wastefully, expanding their inventories, and disregarding the possiblities of materials-saving innovations. Such behaviour, and the resultant permanent excess demand, have been made possible by what Kornai (1979, 1980) calls a 'soft' budget constraint.

This well known system-specific feature strongly influences the resource intensity of Soviet-type economies. As a result, they display much higher resource intensity per unit of output than market economies (MEs) (See Table I/1). Another symptom of the same feature is the low priority of product quality under central planning. It is, however, the high resource intensity that became more significant after the commodity boom of the early 1970s and the two oil shocks. For all East European STEs, except the USSR, it contributed to the worsening of the terms of trade and the growing shortages of energy and industrial raw materials.

Table I/1

RESOURCE INTENSITY OF EAST EUROPEAN STEs AND INDUSTRIALISED WEST EUROPEAN MEs: ENERGY AND STEEL, 1979-80

Countries	Energy intensity in 1979 in kg of coal equivalent consumption per 1000 US dollars[b] of GDP	Steel intensity in 1980 in kg of steel consumption per 1000 US dollars[b] of GDP
East European STEs		
Bulgaria	1464	87
Czechoslovakia	1290	132
Hungary	1058	88
GDR	1356	88
Poland	1515	135
Soviet Union	1490	135
Total, unweighted (6)	1362	111
West European MEs		
Austria	603	39
Belgium	618	36
Denmark	502	30
Finland	767	40
France	502	42
Germany	565	52
Italy	655	79
Norway	1114	38
Sweden	713	44
Switzerland	371	26
United Kingdom	820	38
Total, unweighted (11)	660	42

[b] 1979 US dollars
Sources: World Development Report 1981, Appendix, Tables 1 and 7; *Yearbook of International Statistics*, Warsaw 1982, Table 110 (in Polish). Own calculations.

The importance of this development may be measured by the simple fact that raw materials and intermediate goods account for more than one half and in some cases up to three-quarters of these countries' total imports. Thus an old weakness has become a matter of much greater urgency recently. (It may be added as an aside that this factor is not *the* cause but *a* cause of the decline. Otherwise the USSR, whose terms of trade *improved* both with the West and with the other STEs, ought to have performed better than the rest of Eastern Europe, whose terms of trade worsened.)

INFLEXIBILITY OF HIERARCHY

(2) The inflexibility of the hierarchical multilevel institutional structure of a STE, with commands replacing enterprise initiative, has likewise become an increasingly severe weakness recently. An inordinate amount of (often distorted) information clogs the channels of vertical command and control, creates long lags in the response to disturbances and generally makes central planning a less and less suitable model as economic development progresses. Here the time factor is stressed explicitly but without explaining why the strain on the system has become much greater of late. This is best done by comparing the linkages necessary in 'pure' STE and ME models to produce different types of goods, and then by relating the results to structural change associated with different levels of economic development. Such a comparison[1] shows that the number of linkages is not only markedly higher in STEs than in MEs, but also that it is *increasingly* higher: As an STE moves up the development ladder and shifts its production structure from simple products that need one phase of processing and two enterprises, to products that need many phases of processing and more enterprises related vertically (each receiving inputs and shipping outputs to the next in line) and, finally, to products that need many phases of processing and many enterprises horizontally related (all acting as both suppliers and purchasers of inputs), it requires an increasingly greater number of linkages than MEs.

This result is partially and indirectly supported by comparative input-output analysis,[2] which shows that the complexity of inter-industry linkages increases with the level of economic development. The trend in the world economy during the 1970s and 1980s has been for industries in which vertical relations predominate (steel, cement, bulk chemicals) to be replaced as an engine of growth by industries in which enterprises are typically linked horizontally and act as both suppliers of inputs and purchasers of outputs from each other. These less material-using, more value-adding industries (electrical and non-electrical engineering, instrument making, fine chemicals) where complex, non-linear intra- and inter-industry linkages predominate depend much more for their performance upon features that are the antithesis of central planning.

When STEs started to expand these industries, so that a multitude of new products and more sophisticated versions of old ones began to be manufactured, the sharply increased demands on management became too great a burden for the slow-moving bureaucratic hierarchy and signs of strain multiplied. The shift away from industries based on economies of scale towards those based on innovation and flexibility could be expected to have precisely such consequences and the only surprising thing is that they were not predicted beforehand. It is also interesting to note that the technology imports that were supposed to circumvent the anti-innovative bias of STEs did not help here. On the contrary, the new and higher quality standards of products produced under foreign licences put an additional burden on domestic suppliers of inputs for these products. They also required additional imports, generating extra commands and reports and clogging information channels even further.

STEs reacted to the problems of managing an increasingly complex industrial structure in various — and often contrasting — ways. Hungary, for example, decided to move faster along the road of decentralisation and some reduction in the size of enterprises, while the GDR reinforced controls and created even larger production complexes (combines). Neither of these approaches, however, seems to have led to improved performance, if we judge by the continuing fall in the relative prices obtained by *all* STEs for engineering products on the EEC market in the 1975-80 period. Nor was Bulgaria any more successful, judged either by the same indicator or by Zhivkov's caustic comments on the 'Bulgarisation' of products produced under licence, by which he meant rapid deterioration in quality that accompanies the departure of Western specialists and the substitution of Bulgarian materials, parts, and components for those imported from the West.[3] In more general terms, Hungarian enterprises did not gain enough autonomy and their budget constraint remained soft, while administrative reorganisation in the GDR that made combines less dependent upon other domestic suppliers must have resulted in heavy cost increases and larger inventories (the data on both ceased to be published in the GDR long ago). Thus the possible advantages of organisation have been offset by a reduction in specialisation to a level even lower than normal in STEs.

LACK OF SPECIALISATION

(3) Another system-specific feature of the STEs is what I call the twofold lack of specialisation of their industrial structure.

Owing to their import substitution bias, a result of development policies oriented towards the domestic market, none of the smaller East European STEs realizes the potential advantages of the international division of labour. They turn out too large an assortment of products, especially intermediate products, in too small production runs, with outdated technology and using too many material inputs and factors of production. In consequence, many of these products are costly, technologically obsolete, of low quality and largely uncompetitive on world markets. An important symptom of this lack of specialisation is an overgrown share of industries turning out intermediate products in GDP.

This is not, of course, a feature exclusive to STEs. Many developing countries which chose an import substitution-based strategy have suffered from similar problems. But STEs are saddled with another lack of specialisation, this time purely system-specific. Given the chronic and endemic shortage of everything, enterprises display an extreme do-it-yourself bias. To reduce the uncertainty on the supply side, they prefer to produce as much as possible within their own organisation. They try to do all phases of processing, to make all parts and components for the final product, as well as parts and components and auxiliary instruments for the equipment installed in their plants. As a result, the scale of the enterprise does not equal the scale of production. Labour is spread over too many activities, while intermediate products are produced at a higher cost than would have been the case in specialised enterprises. If the underspecialisation at the country level affects the share of industry indirectly, through the overgrown share of industries producing intermediate goods, the underspecialisation at the enterprise level affects that share directly, since it appears in all industries, increasing the share of industry in GDP. However, the effect is most marked in the engineering industries, where both the number of phases of processing and the quantity of parts and components is by far the largest.

Here again it is possible to point to a source of increased problems in recent years. As the engineering industries have been regarded as a key to the strategy of 'intensive'[4] growth of STEs, their accelerated expansion, reinforced by technology and capital imports, not only increased the problems of management but also created additional demand for resources (labour, capital, material inputs) that were simply beyond the capacity of these economies. But where these demands could not be met in full, there was nevertheless a shift of resources to the engineering industries, which aggravated problems in other sectors.

Another factor should be stressed at this point. The overdevelopment of the industrial sector could proceed as long as labour was available for employment in this sector. But by the late 1970s the source of labour provided by the shift out of agriculture into industry had largely dried up.[5] On the other hand intra-industry movement of labour from slow to fast growing branches in a basically autarkic economy is almost non-existent. Thus industry could look only to increments in the labour force, which had to be shared with the long neglected service sector.

The long neglect of the service sector may have begun to affect the performance of STEs more strongly of late. All the STEs, with the possible exception of Romania, have for the last decade and more been within the GNP *per capita* range associated with the peaking of industry's share and the accelerated increase in the share of services in both GDP and employment. As industry's share continued to grow (Winiecki, 1984b, 1986b), provision of the services required to support industrial growth decreased, precisely when that support was becoming more crucial owing to the rapidly increasing complexity of the industrial sector itself.

SLOWNESS TO INNOVATE

(4) Slowness to innovate is another well known feature of STEs (see the most often quoted Berliner, 1976). We have already stressed the lack of incentives for material inputs-saving innovations, but there is also a more fundamental source of resistance. I have pointed out elsewhere (Winiecki, 1982) that every innovation has to be introduced into existing production facilities. But the personnel operating these facilities is interested, first and foremost, in implementing plan targets for the current planning period. Even if an innovation might result in increased production, the risk of long delay while the technology is mastered, and consequent disturbance to production schedules, would strongly militate against such a move. As there is neither the threat of competition nor that of financial failure to counteract enterprise managers' preference for risk aversion in a shortage-plagued STE, innovation is the exception rather than the rule.[6]

Technology imports (and Western credits) that increased rapidly in the 1970s were supposed to circumvent this barrier to 'intensive' growth in STEs and compensate for the decreasing efficiency of investment. But they were not successful. Whilst it cannot be denied that advanced technology and equipment, even if commissioned late and used less efficiently than in the West, raised productivity in the importing countries, this was achieved at a disproportionately high cost in terms of:

(a) more rapid technological obsolescence of the equipment (that was installed and reached planned capacity after long delay);

(b) higher than usual construction cost overruns (associated with the installation of the more sophisticated equipment);

(c) higher than planned imports of intermediate inputs (due

to the inability to cope with the higher standards even at higher cost);

(d) potential export losses (since, after all these delays, the products manufactured under license reached export markets at a very late stage in the product life cycle).

All these adverse effects were topped by disturbances that spread across national economies as additional resources had to be shifted to heavy industries, which were the main recipients of technology imports. Thus, technology imports contributed more to the arrival of the 'time of troubles' than to the expected shift towards 'intensive' growth.

EFFICIENCY OF RESOURCES

(5) Finally, one of the few advantages of central planning, and probably the most important one, according to almost any textbook on comparative economic systems, has been the ability to mobilise large amounts of financial and other resources and to allocate them for the implementation of large-scale priority projects. This particular feature of central planning made a positive contribution to economic growth during the early industrialisation phase, when industries characterised by major economies of scale were the fastest growing ones.[7] But as the role of growth engine began to be taken over by industries in which innovation, flexibility, risk-taking and other entrepreneurial features are crucial, the advantages of this feature were substantially reduced.

As a general comment on the causes of decline which we have enumerated we may say that changes in economic and technological trends in the world economy since the early 1970s, and policy decisions by STEs themselves, have either exacerbated the negative effects of long-standing weaknesses of Soviet-type economies or reduced the few important advantages they possessed. A range of symptoms, like high resource intensity, decreasing efficiency of investment, an over-expanded industrial sector, increased propensity to import, and inability to export more technologically sophisticated and higher quality manufactures, provides evidence of mounting problems in STEs during this period.

At this stage it seems useful to bring in some additional causes of declining performance. We will not deal here, however, with old problems, the adverse impact of which has not increased of late, even if we may expect it to increase in the future (for example, the long neglected infrastructure), nor with new problems, the impact of which is going to be felt increasingly in the future (for instance pollution in the smaller East European countries). Something we shall consider here, however, is the impact of what Drewnowski (1982) calls 'economic tissue' and Wiles (1982) calls 'imponderables'. Both deal in reality with various aspects of the political and socio-psychological framework for economic activity. The former insists that written and unwritten rules of the economic game are neither known to participants nor observed, and in consequence of the decades of suppression of the truth, eradication of dissent (especially dangerous in economies without the capacity for self-correction) and the repudiation of fairness, the 'tissue' in Soviet-type economies has degenerated, resulting in a spectacular deterioration of performance. The latter points to spreading cynicism and corruption which, after years of broken promises, brought about a widespread feeling in Eastern Europe that 'not just the economy but the whole theocratic system is no good'. (Wiles, 1982, p.11).

MORAL POLITICAL DOUBTS

This author would incline to side with Wiles. All the properties enumerated by Drewnowski adversely affect economic activity in Eastern Europe, but there has been no system-wide deterioration in this respect during the 1970s.[8] It is always difficult to sustain an argument that cumulative effects brought about radical change without explaining why this change did not occur earlier or later. On the other hand Wiles' argument, if circumscribed somewhat and linked to certain effects on performance that have intensified of late, may be defined as a second order cause generated by fundamental causes described earlier.

For East European societies the most important effect of the economic decline has been the stagnation and fall in living standards. Hidden inflation has intensified and so for the first time since the early 1950s has open inflation. The continuing stagnation or fall in living standards that began in the late 1970s may well have convinced people in Eastern Europe that even the modest increases in living standards they have enjoyed since around the mid-1950s are over. Having formed such expectations, societies at large, not only intellectuals, have assumed that the system is hopelessly inefficient (witness the heated discussions on the 'reformability' of the system in Poland in 1980-81).

The effects of such views would certainly be stronger than the usual workers' reactions to increasing disequilibria on the consumer goods market. Reactions to increasing shortages, longer queues and searches for goods in the form of decreased work effort (spending less time on the job and working less diligently) would affect the countries' economies more severely than before.[9] Such expectations transformed into attitudes and thence into deteriorating work effort, once established, became a (second order) cause that begins to exert an independent effect on economic performance. Hopelessness begets cynicism and cynicism begets corruption, contributing directly to a further decline. It matters little that in Poland people would openly say that the emperor has no clothes, in Hungary they would voice cautiously their hope that, maybe, possibly, there is a chance that, after all, the new clothes would eventually be made, and in the remaining countries they would say little or nothing at all on the subject. The differentiating factor would probably be found elsewhere, in the industrial tradition. In countries that industrialised before communist rule, workers and bureaucrats simply would not perform below a certain modest level because they would not think it possible, while in recently transformed peasant societies those levels could be significantly lower.

THE SYMPTOMS: SOME QUANTITATIVE INDICATORS

Let us turn now to symptoms produced by the fundamental causes outlined above. It is at this point that some empirical evidence can be presented and weighed against the claims of recent relative or absolute deterioration of the economic situation in Eastern Europe. Much of the evidence has already been cited elsewhere, so only evidence less often referred to or completely new will be presented here.

HIGH RESOURCE INTENSITY

The most discussed symptom has certainly been *high resource intensity*. Caused by relatively well known system-specific features, it was a characteristic of Soviet-type economies throughout their whole development process. At present the consumption of energy and steel *per* US dollar of GNP is still 2-2.5 times higher than in the industrial West (see Table I/1). Smil and Kuz (1976) formulated the theory that countries pass through three stages of energy intensity in the development process. In the first, pre-industrial stage the energy consumption per unit of GDP is low. Next, as industrialisation progresses, the consumption increases rapidly. Finally, in mature economies, less resource-intensive industries take the lead and the share of industry in GDP slowly declines, while that of services increases. As a result, in the third phase the consumption of energy per unit of GDP decreases. This theory has been confirmed by the development patterns of developing and mature Western economies.

I have compared STEs' present consumption of energy with that of some industrialised West European MEs 20 years earlier, when the latter had GNP *per capita* levels within the range currently exhibited by the STEs (Winiecki, 1983). The results showed that the theory did not hold with respect to STEs: their present energy intensity is much higher. These findings are further confirmed by comparison of the STEs with current data for Ireland

and Spain, countries within the same GNP *per capita* range. Again, the energy intensity of the former was shown to be 1.5-2 times higher than the latter.

While saddled with system-specific high resource intensity,[10] all STEs except the Soviet Union have been facing a relative fall in domestic resource availability. By the end of the 1960s they were all, again except for the Soviet Union, industrial raw materials importers and subsequently became net energy importers as well (with Poland closing the list in the late 1970s). High resource intensity, coupled with growing import needs, has become a serious growth-inhibiting factor. Although the smaller STEs obtained a large part of their imported natural resources from the Soviet Union, the cost of these resources began to increase and this resulted in trade deficits with the Soviet Union too. With resource imports from the Soviet Union not expected to increase substantially (if at all) and the possibility of supply from the world market precluded by their indebtedness and weak export performance, the smaller STEs face a dilemma: they either stagnate and possibly decline or they introduce far-reaching reforms that would reduce resource intensity to the levels found elsewhere. This dilemma is shown graphically in Figure 1. It ought to be stressed

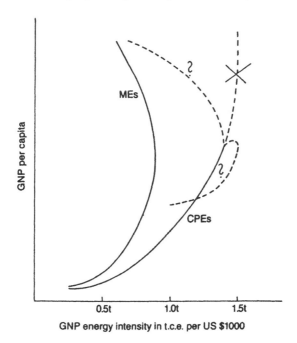

Actual changes in GNP energy intensity of market economies (MEs) and Soviet-type economies (STEs) at different GNP *per capita* levels and alternative future paths of energy intensity available for STEs

that the prospects of reducing natural resource intensity within the system of central planning are not very bright. In 1976-80, when all STEs were beginning increasingly to feel the effects of high resource intensity, four of them (Czechoslovakia, the GDR, Hungary, and Poland) experienced a further increase in resource intensity of net material product, while the decrease in the remaining countries was negligible. Substantial savings were achieved only in the Soviet Union and Bulgaria, and even there only in industry (see *Economic Survey of Europe*, 1982).

DETERIORATING INVESTMENT PERFORMANCE

Deteriorating investment performance is another symptom of deep-seated system-specific causes. Wrongly structured incentives, coupled with the 'soft' budget constraint of enterprises, generate excess demand for capital as well as for everything else. An additional stimulus stems from the reluctance to innovate, which leaves open only one option when attempting to reduce shortages, i.e. more investment. The overgrown industrial sector creates further, self-perpetuating pressure for more investment. Finally, the planning and administrative hierarchy reacts more and more slowly as investment projects become more complex and investment rises faster in industries with rapidly changing technologies.[11]

This long-standing weakness continues to plague STEs in spite of a never ending stream of decrees and policy initiatives aimed at the 'further perfecting of the investment mechanism'. Repeated investment booms and subsequent cutbacks are as much a part of the economic growth pattern now as they were in the past. This is because partial reforms try only to reduce the *absolute* attractiveness of investment. A more successful way would be to reduce the *relative* attractiveness of investment *vis-à-vis* innovation, but that would need far-reaching reforms of the system. As long as the hierarchical bureaucracy of central planning and the 'soft' budget constraint of enterprises remain unchanged, excess demand for investment will flourish no matter what partial reforms are undertaken.

STEs are notorious for their poor investment performance and their economic growth is much more strongly related to *investment effort* than to *investment effects*. Net material product growth rates are much more strongly correlated with investment growth rates without a lag than with a lag of a year or two, thus confirming that *it is the actual process of investing that contributes to economic growth* rather than the effects of earlier investment activity working through into production from new capacity. Not only is this process wasteful, it is becoming *increasingly* wasteful; this is shown by the fact that when we add more recent years, up to 1983, to the time series we find an increase in both the correlation coefficients and the level of significance (see Winiecki, 1986a). As this increasingly wasteful process continued, disequilibria mounted instead of subsiding. Investment cutbacks became necessary during the 1976-80 five-year plan, and investment grew at a lower rate everywhere (in Poland it actually fell). The decrease in investment slowed down economic growth rates to zero or near zero at the start of the 1980s. To save living standards from falling too far, further investment cutbacks were ordered and, even if not fully implemented, brought an absolute decline in investment in most STEs in the early 1980s. (These developments are too well known to require elaboration here.)

The falling efficiency of investment, coupled with constraints on the growth of the volume of investment, do not augur well for the future economic growth of the Soviet Union and the other STEs. As the growth of the labour force slowed down, investment became all the more important as the engine of what is still basically 'extensive' growth. Soviet-type economies are very dependent on high economic growth rates, because the low quality of products and their negligent use and maintenance by the workforce are a substantial cause of excess demand by enterprises, over and above what is generated by other factors we have already analysed. Low quality pipes (rails, etc.) have to be replaced much more often than high quality pipes; low quality roads have to be repaired more often than high quality roads; the same is true of productive equipment. Examples of high turnover of low quality products in STEs abound in the literature. Low quality creates demand for greater quantity, and greater quantity calls for more investment to turn out those low quality products. This and the other factors contributing to excess demand for investment all amount to a considerable upward pressure on the share of investment in NMP.[12] At the same time the ability of STEs to satisfy this demand has been weakening both quantitatively and qualitatively. This cleavage between requirements and abilities is likely to widen in the future as new and/or greater requirements are added to the existing ones.

OVER-EXPANSION OF THE INDUSTRIAL SECTOR

The insatiable demand for everything, not only for investment, will also be more difficult to satisfy in the future because of the over-expansion of the share of the industrial sector in GDP. This particular symptom of STEs has gone almost unnoticed, probably because distorted relative prices in these countries discouraged comparative analysis. The only study of this question with which I am familiar stressed precisely the role of relative prices (lower in agriculture and services, higher in industry) in explaining the difference in the share of industry in GDP between STEs and European MEs (*Economic Survey of Europe*, 1969). That conclusion, which was debatable even in 1969, has since lost whatever validity it may once have possessed.

Elsewhere, I have analysed (Winiecki, 1984b, 1986b) the shares of industry in both GDP and employment in 1965 and 1979 in East European STEs, by selecting a sample of 38 industrialising and industrialised (non-Soviet-type) economies and subsequently predicting the shares of industry in STEs from the so-called Chenery regressions. These regressions were run for the above sample for each year. The share of industry in total employment was used as a control dependent variable to test the claim that it is relative prices that explain all the difference in GDP shares.

The results confirmed the tendency of the already overgrown industrial sector in STEs to grow even further. Industry's share in GDP was much higher than predicted in all the STEs, both for 1965 and 1979 — by 13 and 24 percentage points respectively (unweighted averages for 7 East European STEs). The control dependent variable, the share in total employment, confirmed the tendency, although with smaller differences between actual and predicted shares. The results for 1965 were not unequivocal. Although they showed that on average the actual industry share in employment was higher than the predicted one by four percentage points, they also showed that for two countries, Poland and Romania, the actual share was slightly lower. This nonhomogeneity disappeared, however, between 1965 and 1979. In the latter year the actual share was higher than predicted in all seven STEs, by 11 percentage points (unweighted average).

The STEs may therefore be said to differ markedly from the rest of the world in their pattern of structural change. Normally the share of industry in GDP levels off within a certain range of GNP *per capita* and later begins to decline slowly. In the STEs (which in fact are all within that particular GNP *per capita* range), on the other hand, industry's share tends to continue to grow as GNP *per capita* rises further.

Almost all the fundamental weaknesses of STEs, and especially their twofold lack of specialisation, have the effect of creating a tendency for the continuous growth of the industrial sector beyond any limits known from structural changes in the world economy. The distortions in STEs are by now profound and self-perpetuating. First, an overgrown industrial sector, especially manufacturing, creates excessive demand for material inputs. This, in turn, creates a demand for the expansion of the extractive industries. On average in the 1963-80 period the share of extractive industries in total industry was more than twice as high in the

STEs as in small and medium-sized industrialised MEs, and 1.5-2 times as high as in industrialising MEs at comparable GNP *per capita* levels. Second, a disproportionately high share of extractive and manufacturing industries creates excessive demand for transport services. Generally, the transport intensity of economies, like the share of industry, has a tendency to grow as industrialisation progresses, but, again like the share of industry, stabilises and, finally, decreases. The decrease of transport intensity is usually more pronounced than that of the share of industry. All curves reflecting changes across the GNP *per capita* spectrum (share of industry in GDP and employment, transport intensity) look very much alike for all countries, except STEs. At the same time all these curves look very much alike for STEs[13] as a group, indicating their common, system-specific causes. Both sets of curves are shown in Figure 2.

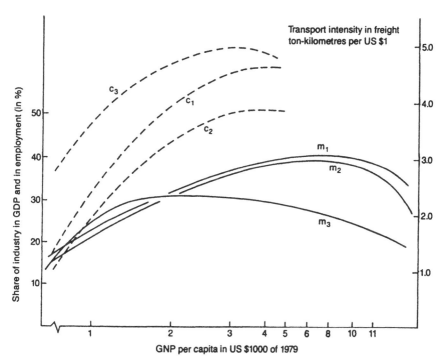

m_1 and c_1 — share of industry in GDP of market (m) and Soviet-type (c) economies
m_2 and c_2 — share of industry in employment
m_3 and c_3 — transport intensity in freight ton-kilometres per unit of GDP ($1 of 1979). Transport intensity of Soviet-type economies excludes the USSR and Romania; transport intensity of market economies includes only European MEs

Trends in the share of industry in GDP and employment related to GNP *per capita* levels in market economies, industrializing and industrialized, and in Soviet-type economies, as well as transport intensity of both, also related to GNP *per capita* levels

This linked pattern of excess demand has profound consequences. Excess demand in manufacturing generates excess demand for investment in the extractive industries and the production of intermediate goods because, allegedly, only investment can alleviate shortages. Pressure for more investment there generates additional demand for investment in the engineering and construction materials industries. This, in turn, generates additional demand for raw materials, basic materials and intermediate goods. At each step excess demand for transport services is generated.

Moreover, as the greatly overgrown industrial sector (which was quite evident by the late 1970s) sucks in a disproportionate share of resources in Soviet-type economies, another kind of adverse effect, already mentioned above, brings pressure to bea upon their performance. The remaining sectors, especially services, understaffed and starved of investment, cannot give the necessary support that the modern industrial economy requires. But it is not only the inadequate infrastructure, like wholesale trade (warehouses, distribution centres), telecommunications and business services, that contributes to the poor performance of STEs. The lack of consumer services raises households' costs, contributing, together with shortages of consumer goods, to the dissatisfaction of the producers as consumers and adversely affecting their work effort.

DETERIORATING FOREIGN TRADE PERFORMANCE

The two remaining symptoms of the deteriorating performance of STEs are related to the external sphere. Over time there has been increasing demand for imports of raw materials, intermediate goods, parts and components. The pattern of excess demand for imports in an import substitution-oriented economy is well known, so it will not be extensively described here. Over time, as new industries are created and their input requirements cannot be satisfied domestically, given the high costs of producing too many goods in too short production runs, the demand for imported material inputs increases rather than decreases. STEs are no exception in this respect. However, they are even more handicapped in the pursuit of their strategies because their excess demand for imports is augmented, first, by their extremely high resource intensity and, second, by the fact that extra supplies can be obtained only from the world market. This is the case because all the STEs pursue the same strategy and all feel the same pressure of demand for imported material inputs.

These pressures have been increased both by the structural changes that have been taking place and by technology imports. We have already indicated that the latter effect was present in all STEs to some extent, whatever the scale of their technology im ports. The ratios of licence-related imports to royalty payments, 8.7:1 for Poland and 12.5:1 for Czechoslovakia, provides partial evidence of this. Attempts to expand the share of engineering industries increased pressure for non licence-related imports across the board in Eastern Europe.

We now turn to the other side of the ledger and look at symptoms of deterioration of export performance on the world (basically Western) market in the period in question. Theoretical arguments leading to the conclusion that the STEs are permanently handicapped by inability to specialize in manufactured exports can be rigorously formulated (see, e.g. Holzman, 1979, and Winiecki, 1985a). The problem is how to substantiate the theory with some evidence.

A good indicator of the degree of processing or of value added is the so-called kilogramme price. As a kilogramme of computers adds, obviously, many times more value than, say, a kilogramme of rails, a price realized in exports *per* kilogramme is to some extent an indicator of the sophistication of the product structure of exports and can be compared with the price realized by another country on a given market or markets.

Engineering products were chosen as the best indicator because all the important ingredients, like innovativeness, flexibility, quality of workmanship, good after-sales service, are needed for success there. Taking the average prices realized by the industrialised West on the EEC market as reference prices, I calculated the ratio of the prices obtained by STEs on the same market to Western reference prices for 1965, 1970 and 1980, as an indicator of disparity in product structure (and let us add, in product quality) in exports to competitive markets.[14]

One important conclusion which can be drawn from the calculations is that all STEs registered relative deterioration of their export prices compared with those obtained by Western countries over the 15 year period: for the STEs as a group the ratio (a weighted average) fell from 0.50 to 0.35, that is to say, whereas in 1965 the average price per kilogramme of STEs engineering products amounted to half the price for those goods realised by Western countries, in 1980 it amounted to about one third. Of even greater importance here is the fact that while in the 1965-70 period two countries improved their relative position slightly (Bulgaria, Romania) and Poland maintained hers, in the 1970-80 period all registered more or less marked deterioration of the ratio.

There are some other indicators, like the ratio of export price to import price for specific products, that tell us whether, on a product-by-product basis, the disparity with the West in the degree of processing is changing. Yet another indicator is the market share of major product groups in Western imports. They all by and large show the same direction of change, namely, for the worse. It is, however, worth noting that the fall in the STEs' market share in Western imports was not uniform. Four East European countries — Hungary, Poland, Romania and the Soviet Union — increased their share in total Western imports of manufacturers between 1970 and 1977, but all four lost between 1977 and 1981 almost as much as they had gained earlier (the remaining three countries registered a fall in their share in both periods). Since it is the former that expanded technology imports to a larger extent than the latter, this seems to indicate that much of the earlier export expansion was dependent on imports from the West: with these falling in the latter period, the STEs could not maintain their share in Western import markets.

AGGREGATE EFFECTS:
MUCH WORSE THAN OFFICIALLY REPORTED

The principal causes of declining performance, manifested by a variety of symptoms, as we have seen, are reflected in aggregate statistical indicators of economic growth, inflation, consumption growth, and indicators of the welfare of the population. These aggregate effects have already been noted by specialists, who are in general agreement that overall growth statistics are now worse than at any time during the period of communist rule.[15] Our discussion could have ended at this point had it not been for the well known fact that the STEs' aggregate statistics have always overstated their performance. In consequence, their recent performance, bad as it appears, has been in reality worse and in some cases *much* worse than officially reported. But assessments of the extent of the overstatement depend on the ability to break down hidden inflation, that typical STE phenomenon (see, e.g. Wiles, 1983, Pindak, 1983, Winiecki, 1982, 1985b), into the component reducing economic growth and that constituting inflation pure and simple. This, in turn, depends upon a proper framework for analysis of hidden inflation.

HIDDEN INFLATION

We begin our analysis of hidden inflation by considering the level of the hierarchy at which the hidden inflation is concealed. Csikos-Nagy, for many years chairman of the Hungarian price commission, stressed in a recent article that in other STEs the sample of goods used to calculate price indices does not include: (a) goods sold on the free (kolkhoz) market, (b) goods produced by small, local market-oriented enterprises and (c) in some STEs not even services sold by the state sector. The *coverage* is thus too narrow. At the same time prices of representative goods remain unchanged and changing weights of different goods, for example an increase in the share of higher priced substitutes, are ignored. The *accuracy* is thus low also.

In consequence, a part of inflation in STEs other than Hungary and, to a lesser extent and more recently, Poland[16] has remained hidden *by design* of the centre. This has regularly distorted the consumer prices index in a downward direction. Beside these regular distortions by design the indices have also been affected by irregular distortions *by fiat*. As the disequilibrium generated by system-specific features accumulated, price increases became necessary. However, their true magnitude has been concealed from the public.[17]

Hidden inflation, however, is not confined to inflation hidden by the centre from the public, but also includes — figuratively speaking — inflation hidden by the public from the centre. Many Eastern and Western authors have shown various ways in which enterprises doctor their reports on plan execution that not only distort quantity statistics upwards — but also price statistics downwards. Three such methods do both at the same time (see, Csikos-Nagy, 1975, and Winiecki, 1982).

(a) The crudest is to change the product mix so as to increase the weight of higher priced substitutes in the output of an enterprise. The advantages for an enterprise are obvious: higher production value allows it to fulfil plan targets more easily or exceed them by some percentage and gain the associated rewards for managers and workers alike. These changes, sometimes known as 'leaching', are·not known to central planners if product mix is changed at the enterprise level, so the comments above by Csikos-Nagy and Racz do not concern *that* part of leaching.

(b) The next is deterioration in the quality of the product, due to shoddy workmanship or sub-standard material inputs (or both). If quality decreases with unchanged prices, the real price level increases, even if the controlled prices of the products concerned do not.

(c) Finally, pseudo-innovations — products whose prices are increased disproportionately more than improvements in their sophistication — raise the price level. This process is often accompanied by the disappearance of less expensive substitutes (leaching).

These three methods of doctoring enterprise statistics have, as we have indicated, a dual impact. They distort price statistics downward, because they increase the price level without increasing prices of particular products controlled by central planners. But they also distort quantity statistics upward, because price increases are registered in the aggregate statistics as quantity increases.

It should be stressed, however, that inflation hidden from

above and from below is often accompanied by what we might call inflation half-hidden from both sides. As disequilibrium increases, central planners may, one way or another, encourage enterprises to increase prices by lowering quality or producing higher priced pseudo-innovations. To give some examples, let us quote, first, two 1972 letters to meat industry enterprises from their superiors ordering them to reduce meat content in sausages by an amount equivalent to a 12.8% price increase (Laski, 1977). Next, it was an open secret in Poland that an unpublished circular letter was sent by the then Prime Minister to all Polish enterprises in 1976 setting the *minimum* price increase for new products in comparison with old substitutes at 30%. This was a roundabout way of mopping up excess demand when officially announced price increases were called off after strikes had erupted. The centre was thus ready to allow itself to be misled to some extent about the real quantity of consumer goods supplied if at the same time equilibrium on the consumer goods market was restored.

Our discussion here has been limited to the consumer prices index and the consumer goods market, but all three methods listed above are also applied to wholesale prices and the producer goods market (see, e.g. Pindak, 1983). It is worth noting that, as a result, central planners know less about real quantities on the producer goods market, which to them is more important, because they do not themselves cheat there but are exclusively cheated against. By contrast, on the consumer goods market they are nearer to true figures because they know by how much they have themselves cheated and they know when they have nudged enterprises to cheat and may at least try to approximate the effects.

Not all manifestations of hidden inflation have the effect of reducing economic growth. But purely fictitious additions to plan fulfilment figures, deterioration in quality as a result of use of sub-standard inputs, as well as pseudo-innovations which boost value added should certainly be subtracted from economic growth rates. How much should be subtracted from growth figures which are already low now is not easy to assess.

EXAGGERATION OF GROWTH RATES

The most extensive cross-national and longitudinal study of this question is the UN Economic Commission for Europe study of GDP *per capita* levels in the West and the East and their rate of change over the 1951-73 period. This showed very characteristic patterns of deviation between the official GDP/NMP data and those obtained by the use of a methodology based on physical indicators.[18]

First, the scale of deviations in MEs (with the exception of

Japan) was markedly smaller than in STEs and, second, the deviations in MEs were in *both* directions, while in the STEs the deviations were not only larger but in *one direction only*, that is the growth rates based on physical indicators were in all cases lower than the officially reported ones. Only Hungary displayed deviations that remained within the range typical for MEs (showing again that its statistics are the most reliable in Eastern Europe). The comparisions for all 7 STEs for the whole 1951-73 period considered in the study, as well as for the respective subperiods, are reproduced in Table I/2. They show that the more realistic economic growth rates in STEs calculated on the basis of the methodology employed in the UN study constituted between 90% (Hungary) and 55% (GDR) of the officially reported ones (the use of *per capita* rather than overall growth rates does not affect the comparison much), But even these ratios may be biased upwards. In my view the methodology of the UN study is not able to capture all the growth-reducing effects of hidden inflation. Quality deterioration caused by shoddy workmanship and the use of sub-standard material inputs passes undetected and forced replacement purchases of such goods (because of their rapid deterioration) are counted as volume growth of production and/or consumption. Also, the rates of growth of goods and services other than those on the list of physical indicators are assumed to be lower by the same percentage, which need not necessarily be the case.

More highly differentiated products lend themselves more easily to doctoring than, for example, steel, cement, cars or sugar (all on the list of physical indicators).

That we are on the right track may be seen from a larger, painstakingly detailed study of Soviet economic growth prepared for the US Congress (J.E.C., 1982). Using an eclectic methodology comprising time series on consumption or production in volume terms and official time series in value terms where more reliable data could not be obtained, as well as a much larger number of products and product groups, the authors' calculations yielded a GNP growth rate over the 1951-80 period that constituted some 63.5% of the officially reported NMP growth rate (4.7% compared with 7.4%). Thus a larger coverage resulted in a greater differential between a realistically calculated growth rate and an officially reported one (a reduction for the Soviet Union from 71.6% to 63.5%). Significantly, the authors of the JEC study maintain that if their calculated growth rates are biased, the bias is in an *upward* direction.

Thus the falling economic growth rates of the recent period may in fact be by some 10% to 45% lower than the official figures, or even by more. But the story does not end here. These subtractions from official growth rates are averages for long periods. The question is to what extent Nove's 'law of equal cheating', that the differential between real and reported growth rates (Nove, 1977) is unchanged, is really valid. A tentative answer on the basis of Table I/2 is that it is valid to a very limited extent (if at all).

Table I/2

DIFFERENCES BETWEEN GNP *PER CAPITA* GROWTH RATES BASED ON PHYSICAL INDICATORS, AS ESTIMATED IN THE UN STUDY, AND OFFICIAL NMP *PER CAPITA* RATES ACCORDING TO NATIONAL STATISTICS OF STEs

	Bulgaria	Czecho-slovakia	GDR	Hungary	Poland	Romania	USSR
1950-55	7.2	3.7	5.2	5.3	4.1	5.7	5.1
UN	7.2	3.7	5.2	5.3	4.1	5.7	5.1
O	8.1	6.9	13.7	4.6	6.6	12.6	9.1
diff.	−0.9	−3.2	−8.5	0.7	−2.5	−6.9	−4.0
1956-60							
UN	7.9	4.5	4.7	4.0	3.9	4.9	5.2
O	8.7	6.2	8.0	5.7	4.8	5.6	7.7
diff.	−0.8	−1.7	−3.3	−1.7	−0.9	−0.7	−2.5
1961-65							
UN	7.4	4.0	3.5	5.1	4.8	7.5	5.4
O	5.9	1.1	3.7	3.7	4.7	8.3	5.1
diff.	1.5	2.9	−0.2	1.4	0.1	−0.8	0.3
1966-70							
UN	6.1	3.7	3.2	5.0	4.7	5.8	4.4
O	8.0	6.5	5.1	6.5	5.1	6.5	6.5
diff.	−1.9	−2.8	−1.9	−1.5	−0.4	−0.7	−2.1
1971-73							
UN	3.4	3.5	3.4	4.5	5.5	5.8	3.9
O	7.2	4.5	5.4	6.3	9.7	10.2	5.1
diff.	−3.8	−1.0	−2.0	−1.8	−4.2	−4.4	−1.2
1950-1973							
UN	6.6	3.9	4.0	4.8	4.5	5.9	4.8
O	7.6	5.0	7.2	5.3	5.9	8.5	6.7
diff.	−1.0	−1.1	−3.2	−0.5	−1.4	−2.6	−1.9
UN/O	0.868	0.780	0.556	0.906	0.763	0.694	0.716

UN   = estimates based on physical indicators
O   = official accounts
diff. = difference in growth rates in percentage points
UN/O= ratio of volume based to officially reported NMP growth rates

Source: *Economic Bulletin for Europe*, Vol. 31, No. 2 (1980)

The best example is provided by the STE with the most distorted statistics, namely the GDR. Realistic growth rates for the 1950-55 and 1961-65 periods constituted 38% and 94.6% of the officially reported ones respectively. The extremely high differential in the earlier period can be explained by the propaganda needs of the communist regime which thought it necessary to demonstrate — at least on paper if not in reality — superior performance in comparison with the West German 'Wirtschaftswunder'. As the Federal Republic's economic growth rates, both overall and *per capita*, were very high then, the very large overstatements of actual rates were needed to show the communist system's 'supremacy'. On the other hand, the extremely low differential for 1961-65 may be related to the 'New Economic System', the only experiment with some decentralised economic management in the GDR's history, that required among other things improved statistics to avoid misleading the country's own authorities.

There is not much evidence for the most recent period. However, I regard it as another period of extremely high differentials between very low real NMP growth rates and officially reported ones in the GDR. Many of the available input-output ratios are wildly off their trend values and all the partial indices of repressed inflation on the consumer goods market also point strongly in this direction. The aim of these large overstatements is also political: to show that the GDR, the stalwart of central planning orthodoxy, is immune to the marked economic decline visible elsewhere in Eastern Europe. The change from the need to prove supremacy over the Federal Republic to the need to prove merely the ability to avoid decline in itself says a lot about the lowered expectations in Eastern Europe.

Again, partial support for the hypothesis can be found in the recent study by Alton (1985) on changes in East European GNP since 1970. According to his estimates East German GNP growth rate in the 1975-1982 period was only 49.5% of the official NMP growth rate (15.6% vs. 31.5% respectively for the period as a whole). With all the usual reservations as to the degree of comparability of GNP and NMP, it is an overstatement higher than average for the 1950-1973 period in the U.N. study and lower only than that for the 1950-1955 subperiod there. It is worth noting, though, that for one country the overstatement was markedly higher. This country was not Romania (as might have been expected) but Bulgaria whose estimated growth was equal to only 23% of the official one [sic!].

In general, except for Poland, the differentials between official East European data and Alton's estimates were higher — from 44.4% to 77% — than in the U.N. study for the 1950-1973 period. The ranking of countries according to differentials was also different from the latter, with Bulgaria and GDR at the top, i.e. with higher overstatements, and Poland at the bottom, i.e. with the least distorted growth statistics.[19]

Nor does the law of equal cheating find much support in the case of the other STEs in Table I/2, or in individual country studies. It is clear from Table I/2 that most STEs had higher differentials at the beginning and at the end of the period covered. Country studies confirm this picture. The 1982 JEC study shows the highest differentials for the Soviet Union in 1951-55, 1971-75 and 1976-80; the golden period of honesty in reporting was 1961-65, as in Table I/2. Similarly, Askanas and Laski have shown that there was an acceleration of hidden inflation and a rise in the differential in the 1970s compared with the 1960s in Poland in the case of consumer goods and services (Askanas and Laski, 1985). Thus we may hypothesize that, with mounting problems, the temptation to doctor statistics both at the enterprise level — to show plan fulfilment — and at the centre — to show better aggregate performance — has been on the increase.

It is of interest to ask to what extent the slightly better performance of the Soviet economy in 1985-86 is the result of an increasingly more imaginative reporting in response to a more energetic cracking of the whip by the new boss. There has been a strong correlation between impaired official figures and increased complaints of doctored statistics by Soviet officials. It was revealed in a 1981 article by a deputy chairman of the Soviet People's Control Committee that about one-third of checked-up enterprises had been caught cheating in their plan implementation reports (*Planovoe Khozyaistvo*, 1981, No.11). It may reasonably be expected that all figures have increased, that is the size of over statements, the number of those cheating, and the number of those caught cheating. Many more may be punished nowadays but, in an almost stagnant economy, plan fulfillment becomes increasingly difficult and consequently returns to cheating are also higher than in the good old days of (moderately!) high growth.

The modest improvement in growth figures in STEs since 1983 does not change the picture substantially for several reasons. *First*, the growth figures are much overstated, and they are most overstated in the countries showing the highest official growth. *Second*, debt repayment will continue to exert strong pressure upon aggregate supplies by diverting a sizeable share of consumer goods in the smaller STEs to Western and Soviet markets. *Third*, investment has already begun to rise again and, although a return to the high growth rates of the era before the late 1970s is well-nigh impossible, a shift of resources away from consumption and toward investment is on the way and will strengthen the tendency to falling consumption. In the STE system this is more production growth for the sake of production growth. *Fourth*, in view of the character of the Soviet-type system, economic growth at the rate that may be regarded as realistic seems unlikely to be sufficient to ensure even the replacement of capital stock, infrastructure and installation of the most urgently needed anti-pollution equipment. Under the circumstances stagnation of economic growth and falling consumption become a norm rather than an exception. And the consequence of that will be particularly serious for a system which derives its legitimacy exclusively from a 'further, ever fuller satisfaction of the material needs of the working people', the obligatory slogan in all STEs.

I.3. CONSTRAINTS ON FUTURE OPTIONS

If stagnation or decline is what STEs face in the 1980s and beyond, then various actions aimed at remedying the situation may be expected to be undertaken by the ruling communist elites in these countries. In this section I preface my future-oriented discussion of what are the probable (or only possible) developments in Eastern Europe with an analysis of the constraints under which the ruling elites operate or, more simply, of what they *cannot* do to improve the situation.

To begin with, they cannot initiate and sustain for long another large-scale investment expansion. Although investment exceeded plan targets in the 1981-84 period (the plans provided for even larger cutbacks), it grew at much lower rates than at any time in the past. An investment drive would sharply curtail consumption, which so far has been cushioned in most countries precisely by the reduction in investment. A serious fall in living standards would threaten the rulers' goals either directly, through the eruption of discontent, or indirectly, through falling morale and decreased effort by the labour force, a spreading belief in the absence of prospects for improvement, and reinforced cynicism about the entire system.

However, the nature of a STE demands continuing high investment and production growth rates. The shortfall of the last few years will make itself felt in due course in the East European economies. Although scattered data for some STEs on the age structure of equipment (especially in Poland, Hungary, with Czechoslovakia and the Soviet Union not very much behind) show signs of deterioration. But it should be remembered that industry, both mining and manufacturing, has always been a priority area. It is in the infrastructure, which has been neglected more than ever recently, that the signs of deterioration are going to be visible (with Poland again in the forefront).

If the economies are not to grind to a halt, the share of infrastructure investment would have to increase in any investment expansion, whether on a large or a modest scale. Given the speed of deterioration infrastructure must soon take a larger share of investment whether the latter increases or not. Moreover, there is still another claimant on investemnt; ecological problems will not go away. On the contrary, they will intensify. So far, as we have already pointed out, these problems have by and large been 'solved' by being ignored. This neglect cannot be continued much longer, particularly in the smaller East European countries. Already central and southern Poland, the GDR and the Czech lands constitute the most polluted area of the world.

ECOLOGICAL PROBLEMS

Eastern Europe, except the Soviet Union, emitted in 1982 some 40.7 mill. ton of sulphur dioxide as compared to 18.6 mill. ton for the EEC countries. The above figures are more poignant if one takes into account that East European countries have a slightly smaller territory, a significantly lower population, a much smaller industrial production and very much lower living standards. On *per capita* basis emissions in GDR are over four times higher than in W. Germany! While emissions in Czechoslovakia as a whole are only a little lower than those in GDR, those in the Czech part of that country are markedly higher (see, e.g. *Ambia*, 1982, and Postel, 1984). Other sources of pollution, as well as damage caused by mining, are also much higher than in the West. Even a slowdown in the rate of degradation of land, forest and town habitats will cost a lot.

Given these constraints and the deteriorating efficiency of investment, I see no possibility of an investment expansion large enough and lasting enough to increase production sufficiently to avoid stagnation in real terms. As economic growth figures are distorted by hidden inflation and quality deterioration, an 'official' economic growth rate of at least 5% annually would be needed to improve the situation slightly. But even this rate, which does not look very probable, would be insufficient to halt the decline in living standards. Too large a share of investment would have to go to infrastructure and the manufacture of investment and intermediate goods. The decline in living standards would further undermine the performance of the workforce, making the maintenance of such a high rate completely out of the question in the longer term.

The old-style solution is all the more unattainable because the East European economies simply lack the material inputs necessary to pursue the traditional resource-intensive strategy. Even the Soviet Union now finds expansion of its resource base exceedingly costly and is unable to expand it in spite of huge investment in the extraction of most important fuels (oil, coal) and some industrial raw materials. The smaller countries, indebted to the West and registering regular trade deficits with the USSR, are even more tightly constrained.

Table I/3

INPUTS FOR TECHNOLOGICAL CHANGE IN EAST AND WEST: R AND D SHARE IN GDP EXPENDITURES AND SCIENTISTS AND ENGINEERS IN R AND D ESTABLISHMENTS AND IN TOTAL EMPLOYMENT AS A PERCENTAGE OF TOTAL EMPLOYMENT (EXCLUDING AGRICULTURE) AT THE END OF THE 1970s

	R and D as a percentage of GDP in 1979	R and D personnel as a percentage of total employment (excluding agriculture)[a]	Scientists and engineers as a percentage of total employment (excluding agriculture)[a]
East European STEs			
Bulgaria	1.7 (1977)[b]	1.5	8.2
Czechoslovakia	2.9 (1978)[b]	1.8	5.4[c]
Hungary	2.5 (1978)[b]	1.4	9.3
GDR	—	2.2	6.3
Poland	1.6 (1978)[b]	1.4	6.9[d]
Romania	—	0.7	—
Soviet Union	3.4 (1977)[b]	—	11.6
Western MEs			
Canada	0.9	0.5	7.6
Finland	—	0.8	9.3
France	1.8	1.3	9.2
FRG	2.3	1.0	5.3[b]
Italy	0.8	0.5	7.0
Japan	2.0	1.4	11.5
Sweden	1.9	1.0	—
United Kingdom	2.2 (1978)	—	—
United States	2.4	0.8	3.2

[a] R and D personnel and scientists and engineers around 1977; total employment in 1976.

[b] Estimated from NMP data according to UN ECE methodology.

[c] Scientists and engineers in 1973.

[d] Scientists and engineers in 1970.

Sources: Rocznik statystyki miedzynarodowej, 1981, Warsaw, Tables 62, 317, 319; *ibid.* 1977, Table 277; H. Giersch, F. Wolter, 'Towards an Explanation of the Productivity Slowdown: An Acceleration-Deceleration Hypothesis', *Economic Journal*, 93, (1983) p.41; author's calculations.

Thus the quantities of production factors and material inputs necessary to resume relatively fast economic growth and consumption growth in real terms are largely out of reach for East European countries. But what about the quality of inputs and factors of production? All over Eastern Europe now one finds official declarations of the necessity 'to catch up with the technologically most advanced countries'. But without far-reaching reforms that would remove the fundamental causes of the resistance to innovation a quality breakthrough is beyond reach.

TRANSLATION OF INVENTIONS INTO INNOVATIONS

The usual solution, quantitative expansion, this time of research and development effort, will not succeed because it is the translation of inventions into innovation in production that remains the principal obstacle. Besides, it is often forgotten that the East already spends *at least* as large a share of its GDP on R and D as the West does. Also, the proportion of R and D personnel in total employment is larger in the former than in the latter. Nor is the population of scientists and engineers in total employment lower in the East than in the West, as Table I/3 shows. The problem is not one of inputs, then, but of outputs in an environment hostile to innovation.

QUALITY

Significant improvements in the quality of output as another way of economizing on inputs is beyond STEs' reach as well. As this author explained elsewhere (Winiecki, 1986a) the above statement should not be construed to mean that STEs are completely unable to produce goods of normal or even high quality. Indeed, Soviet weaponry, as well as some East European manufactures exported to the West, prove that they can. The point I want to make is that system-specific reasons prevent STEs from producing normal, i.e. world standard, quality goods at a normal cost. The military products and goods for export that are made to meet lower-to-medium world quality standards entail a high extra cost in terms of both higher quality material inputs (or the screening of a much larger quantity) and additional labour inputs in assembly, finishing, quality control, and packaging.

A popular myth among central planners and their political masters (as well as many orthodox economists in Eastern Europe) is that the basic cause of the quality problem is excess demand and that excess supply would bring a great improvement. Accordingly, they press for even larger quantity increases. This view is entirely mistaken: On the infrequent and shortlived occasions that there has been an excess supply of some consumer goods, the market was flooded with goods of equally poor quality as under conditions of excess demand.

The reasons for the lack of quality improvement should have been obvious from the start. Without scarcity prices serving, among other things, to differentiate between products of different quality, without hard budget constraints forcing enterprises to stop unwanted production under the threat of bankruptcy and, last but definitely not least, without domestic and foreign competition coupled with hard budget constraint combining to put pressure on enterprises to raise product quality, nothing will change for the better. The bureaucratic measures and propaganda campaigns beloved by communist apparatchiks are of no help. Neither new laws on product quality or declarations of party plenary meetings on the need to pay more attention to quality will change established practices in the STEs in the absence of market discipline. The increasing frequency of such exhortations is another signal of the growing problems STEs face in this area.

Yet another way of improving economic performance, structural change is closed to STEs. Their fast economic growth in the past was mainly the result of two major shifts. First, there was the shift from lower productivity agriculture to higher (even if not impressively high) productivity industry. Second, there was above average growth of those industries that enjoyed economies of scale. Although in four out of seven East European STEs (Bulgaria, Poland, Romania and the Soviet Union) the share of agriculture in employment in 1979 was still higher than that predicted from their development level and size (see Winiecki, 1984b), further possibilities of changing the structure of employment are measured by their costly and inefficient agriculture. Moreover, industry in STEs already employs too large a share of the labour force, so a further increase there is not even desirable (despite industry's clamourings for more workers).

The last possibility of acceleration of economic growth, beside investment expansion, technological change and structural change, especially for the smaller, trade-dependent STEs is greater participation in the international division of labour. However, because their system constrains their ability to specialise in manufactured products they export increasingly scarce commodities, low value-added intermediate products and low quality finished manufactures (often sold at a heavy discount), without taking proper advantage of international specialisation.

But all of them, with the sole exception of the Soviet Union, are net importers of fuels and raw materials. Although they are net exporters of them *vis-à-vis* the West, these possibilities will be increasingly constrained. An important contributing factor is the

Soviet stagnant and prospectively declining oil output that, coupled with lower export earnings in hard currencies due to the fall of price, is expected to limit further supplies to smaller East European countries.

Next, demand for low-value-added intermediate products in the West is expected to remain almost level due to the material-saving technological revolution taking place outside the STEs. Also, there are limits to price discounts offered to increase sales volume not only because of the threat of anti-dumping proceedings but also due to low returns — even in hard currencies — of such strategy. Already prices obtained on the Western markets for, e.g., steel or polymerization products are markedly lower than those obtained by newly industrializing countries. The STEs are clearly losing in competition with the latter countries on the Western markets (see, e.g. Poznanski, 1986).

And to complete the quick survey both STEs' prices and market shares in OECD countries have been decreasing: the former since the mid-1960s and the latter since the late 1970s (see Winiecki, 1985a, and Poznanski, 1986). It is highly doubtful that more sophisticated manufactures would be able to compensate for the declining or stagnant earnings of traditional exports. Competitiveness of STEs' manufactured products continues to be low and, in all probability it is going to decline further. Even the most industrially advanced East Germany seems to be at its best in supplying water to and taking sewage from West Berlin, as well as repairing roads leading to and from that city, rather than in showing its prowess in sophisticated engineering exports on Western markets.

Nor are the STEs any more fortunate in their intra-COMECON trade. Throughout the literature (and, more obliquely, in the utterances of decision makers) the parallel autonomous development of the East European economies has repeatedly been stressed (see, e.g., Nosoczy, 1983). The much vaunted 'reorientation' toward intra-COMECON trade, meant to be a remedy that would help to overcome the constraint on imports from the West, will remain largely an illusion, not only because there is little real specialisation within Eastern Europe, but also because of the differing East-East and East-West import structures. All STEs buy similar products in the West and imports from other STEs are not a substitute in this respect. Also, imports from the West are a safety valve for all STEs when unplanned imports become an urgent necessity, usually in the expansion phase of an investment cycle. As all STEs go through these cycles, all of them experience a similar expansion of demand at approximately the same stage of the five-year plan. Consequently they cannot play the safety valve role for each other, even if one disregards their usual inflexibility and the long lead times necessary to implement contracts. On the contrary, domestic production often has to replace substandard or delayed imports from other East European STEs (see, e.g., Csaba, 1983, for GDR and Hungary). We should also remember that any large volume increase in exports of commodities and intermediate products, that is to say the traditional quantity expansion drive in the external sphere, would come up against the ceiling of resource availability. Even the Soviet Union is increasingly limited in this respect.

In conclusion, on the one hand, continuation of the old wasteful 'extensive' growth is impossible because of constraints on quantities of production factors and material inputs. On the other hand, qualitative changes in the East European economies (innovation, quality improvement, structural change, greater international division of labour) are impeded by the system's inherent constraints. It is this perception of the lack of any prospects for the continuation of the traditional Soviet-type growth model, coupled with the sharply curtailed possibilities of its prolongation by means of Western credits, which led some scholars, both in the East and in the West, to believe that reforms are inevitable. This view is very optimistic, however, as it does not take into consideration certain vital determinants of any remedial action: knowledge of the reality, knowledge of alternatives and, last but surely not least, interest in maintaining the systemic *status quo*, even with — up to a point — falling living standards.

1.4. POSSIBLE SCENARIOS

ALTERNATIVE ONE: FROM OBVIOUS TO LESS OBVIOUS NON-SOLUTIONS

Something which is quite often not appreciated is the low learning capacity of the Soviet-type system. If by learning we mean change in reaction to unchanged actions (stimuli), then learning by a system in which all dissent has been eliminated (or its outward signs suppressed) has been shown to be agonizingly slow. Overvaluation of the ruling elites' collective memories and corresponding undervaluation of incoming current information adversely affect the capacity to recognise the problem, while the narrowing of information inflow decreases the capacity to select a solution. All this affects the system adversely, quite apart from the fact that proposed solutions may run contrary to the ruling elite's interest in maintaining the *status quo* — question to which we return in the next section.

The signs of the exhaustion of expansion possibilites began to appear in Eastern Europe in the early 1960s. Attempts at partial economic reforms in the late 1960s, even if limited, did inject some new vigour into these economies and, with production factors still available in large quantities and natural resources relatively inexpensive, a renewed acceleration of the traditional, wasteful type of growth occurred. In the early 1970s Western technology and credits were substituted for economic reforms. The fact that the exhaustion of expansion possibilities has since reappeared with much stronger symptoms, due both to the decreasing rate of growth of availability of factors of production and much dearer natural resources, does not guarantee that some obvious non-solutions will not be proposed and attempts at their implementation not undertaken. Such developments have actually been taking place for some time in certain East European countries.

'DOWN PERISCOPE' SCENARIO

Two scenarios of this sort can be envisaged, in fact. The first we would call the 'down periscope' scenario. Both the frame of mind of the ruling elites and their reactions to the stimuli can be deduced from its title. Overvaluation of the elites' memory of the 'good old days' and undervaluation of unpleasant current information degenerates, in extreme cases, into a kind of withdrawal symptom. The facts indicate that things are bad and getting worse. If we disregard them, problems may go away. And even if they do not, let us enjoy both the power and the wealth we still have. Moreover, let us eradicate any statements reminding us of the unpleasant problems in question, for if nobody states openly that the emperor has no clothes, then, by convention, the emperor is well clad. And let us repeat on all possible occasions the litany of advantages the system possesses in comparison with any competing one.

In such a scenario grotesque propaganda reigns supreme while nothing really changes in the economic system (the sphere from which the hard data on the deterioration come). The late Gierek era in Poland is a good example of a 'do nothing, pretend the problems do not exist' attitude. This complacency could last, however, as long as Poland's borrowing ability and ceased abruptly in 1980. In this scenario at least some measures are taken, but they are mainly non-economic in character. Exhortations become more and more frequent, campaigns against absenteeism, shoddy goods and black market activities become more shrill, as symptoms are treated (often in all seriousness) as causes of the decline. New layers of control are created and enmeshed with the existing ones and *ad hoc* shock therapies applied, like searches in public places to find people who ought to have been at their respective workplaces (these were instituted in Poland during the early martial law period and then in the Soviet Union at the beginning of Andropov's period of power).

In the management of the economy 'more of the same' still seems to be a frequent resort. Czechoslovakia, for example, carried out another unsuccessful drive to make enterprises adopt more 'taut' plans in the late 1970s and a phony reform that changed nothing in the early 1980s. Everywhere, except in Hungary, one hears about the need to strengthen the role of medium-term plans, as if repeated investment cycles had not shown their untenability. Learning capacity is indeed very low and Pavlovian reflexes dominate the way the system reacts to repeated, although increasingly strong, stimuli.

Even some partial reforms aimed at improving the performance of the increasingly inflexible multi-level hierarchical organization of the economy may be cautiously undertaken, modifying (usually not very consistently) certain less decisive elements of the traditional Soviet-type model. But given the preponderance of the elements of the traditional model they are unable to bring about any discernible and lasting improvment. On the contrary, they may even become a source of new disturbances.

Under the circumstances of the 'down periscope' scenario, performance has nowhere to go but down. All the causes that have been contributing to its deterioration so far are still present, while the cynicism and accompanying corruption spread further. The elites have nothing to offer to the population at large: consumption is falling or stagnant, the conditions of acquiring goods and services are getting worse as disequilibria increase. Moreover the population is not willing to 'swallow' the ideology any more. (Neither the ruled nor the rulers belive it any more. A.J. Toynbee, tracing the sources of the breakdown of civilizations, found that failure voluntarily to imitate the behaviour patterns demonstrated or suggested by the ruling elites usually preceded failure to obey.) In the Soviet-type system the control and repression are so strong that failure to obey may appear only after a relatively long lag. But when the demonstrated behavioural patterns of the ruling elite deviate consistently from the suggested ones a 'reverse mimesis' begins to take place. The population adapts itself to the existing conditions and imitates the demonstrated behavioural patterns of the elite only too well, with corroding effects on the system (and on itself). Thus, whether one begins with the repeated disappointements due to the inferior and deteriorating performance of the economic system, or with the deteriorating integrity of the elites, the outcome is predictable and the same: cynicism and corruption. A second order, but lasting and self-reinforcing, cause of the economic decline has taken root in the body social. There is no need to outline here the step-by-step development under this scenario.

Both the causes-symptoms-effects linkages and the constraints on the 'more of the same' type of response allow us to predict in sufficient detail the dynamics of slow decline.

'RECENTRALISATION-CUM-REPRESSION' SCENARIO

But what if the decision makers decide to apply a large dose of the old medicine, to recentralise decisions and repress those who protest or only dissent? The 'recentralisation-cum-repression' scenario would lead, in my opinion, after a short acceleration due more to imaginative reporting from below than increased effort, to faster decline. As in the previous scenario, all the causes contributing to the decline would be present, but their impact, or at least the impact of some of them, on economic performance would become stronger. Let us begin with the feasibility of the recentralisation part of this scenario. With gross national product now many times greater than in the earlier period of extreme centralisation, during the forced industrialisation in the 1950s, and with a more sophisticated structure of production, the earlier level of centralisation simply cannot be repeated. To give an example, the Czechoslovak economy produces over 5 million products, finished and intermediate. The number of decisions concerning production factors and material inputs to produce each product is far beyond what can be decided consistently at the top of the hierarchical pyramid with the speed necessary to achieve planned production targets (leaving aside the allocational efficiency of such decisions). Nor is it possible at intermediate levels of the hierarchy. It is worth remembering that recentralisation reactions historically have followed the failure of attempts at partial decentralisation of decision making to the middle levels of the hierarchy (but not to the enterprise). Under these circumstances the decision-making process would slow down to a snail's pace.

The next issue to be considered is the non-economic consequences of the 'great (investment) leap forward' that would become a key component of this scenario. Rapid growth in the share of investment would result, under the existing circumstances, in an absolute fall in consumption, or an accelerated fall if consumption were falling already. Would such a fall generate Toynbee's 'failure to obey', open eruption of discontent? It is difficult to answer this question with a high degree of probability. Polish and Romanian experience so far suggests different answers. The limitation to the present is legitimate. For in both cases the fall in living standard has occurrred in spite of cuts in investment (much more drastic in Poland). Thus the negative consumption effects of any large-scale investment expansion would come on living standards which were already falling.

If an open eruption of discontent is a probable, but not a certain outcome of the 'recentralisation-cum-repression' scenario (given the efficiency of the repression), there are other outcomes, well known from past and present, that would certainly contribute to the accelerated decline. The reactions of producers-consumers would, however, be more accentuated than in the earlier case of slow decline and would result in a precipitous fall in the quality of manufactured products. Under the double impact of sharply reduced import possibilities and falling quality, exports of manufactures to world markets would suffer disproportionately. The export structure would resemble that of less entrepreneurial developing countries due to the more than usually dominant role of commodities. Given the fact that commodities would become scarcer and their production more costly, the limits would quickly be reached in the external sphere too. An alternative to exporting more manufactures would be to increase exports of certain commodities (food, fuels) to an even greater extent at the cost of further cuts in consumption, but here, again, the question of possible eruption of discontent has to be taken into account, for it is assumed that there are limits to cuts in living standard below which the fear of repression ceases to be a deterrent (although the threshold may be different in each country).

All in all, the above scenario may be regarded as a short- to medium-run one. It is doubtful whether the kind of developments described could last, in the face of much stronger constraints than before, beyond one investment cycle without a serious breakdown (economic, social or both). And even if the 'down periscope' scenario could be envisaged as a longer lasting one, it is obvious that both are non-solutions to the problem of decline.

THE HUNGARIAN SCENARIO

Yet another scenario is the Hungarian one, that is a more serious attempt at economic reform of the Soviet-type model without relevant changes in the political and social environment in which a reformed model has to function. With respect to the Hungarian scenario, held up sometimes as an example of the reformability of a STE, we have to consider two questions instead of one, as was the case with the previous scenarios. Before ascertaining whether it is possible to repeat it, it is worthwhile considering whether it is desirable, that is, whether it is a clear enough success to be worth emulation.

In my opinion the Hungarian economy since 1968 cannot be regarded as an unqualified success, in spite of the good press it has enjoyed both in the West (due to brilliant salesmanship by Hungarian officials and experts) and (to an extent) in the East. It is true that in macroeconomic terms the level of disequilibrium in the consumer goods market has been smaller than elsewhere. It is also true that its input-output characteristics, like the material intensity of the national economy, are somewhat better than those of other East European countries. Another point in favour of Hungary is its agricultural sector, which since the 1960s has been a significant exporter — and this without simultaneously impoverishing the domestic market (as other food exporters in Eastern Europe do). Yet another difference, since 1980, has been an enhanced entrepreneurial (and, to a much lesser extent, also innovative) vigour on the part of Hungarians, mainly visible in the development of intra-enterprise production initiatives by employees and, to a smaller extent, in new small business establishments, both cooperative and private.[20]

On the other hand, system-specific features continue to affect Hungarian economic performance adversely. Disequilibria, although smaller, still add discomfort to constraints on the level of consumption. Input-output characteristics, better, as we have stressed, than in other STEs, are nevertheless very much higher than in most MEs. A substantial number of large industrial enterprises, inflexible and shunning innovation, are chronically unprofitable. The enterprises that needed relief in 1972 were found in the same situation in 1982, receiving large subsidies, tax reductions and other forms of assistance (see, e.g., Csaba, 1983). It comes as no surprise then that export performance on world markets is not at all impressive as far as manufactures are concerned and small surpluses on trade with the West have been achieved mainly by the familiar method of import cuts. Actually, if it had not been for the favourable view of Hungarian economic reforms taken by Western governments and banks, Hungary might have followed the path of other STEs that asked for debt repayment relief (just as, at the other end of the reform continuum, the West German 'umbrella' helped the GDR to avoid a similar necessity at the peak of the latter's debt repayment burden).

In consequence the Hungarian economy is not reducing the gap in development between itself and the West. On the contrary, in comparison with countries like Austria, Italy and France, or medium-developed Spain, the distance seems to have increased since the late 1920s. Also, the newly industrialising countries (NICs) have been performing much more impressively in the last 15-20 years.

The Hungarian economy is therefore a *qualified* success, the most important qualification being its geopolitical limitation: it is a success relative to other STEs only. This precariousness of the Hungarian position is best understood by those Hungarian economists who know what makes their economy tick. They are concerned that without keeping up the momentum of far-reaching economic reforms, and extending reforms beyond the purely economic area, the gap in development between Hungary and the medium-developed and developed market economies may increase. Very often they voice their concern, even if more obliquely, about all East European countries (see, in particular Kemenes, 1979 and Bognar, 1982).

Nonetheless, Hungarian attempts at economic reform have certainly been serious by East European standards. The first phase, beginning in 1968 and severely handicapped after a few years, was indeed modest, but the second phase that started in 1980 together with the 'second-plus' phase in 1984 brought some important changes. On the institutional side it all but abolished the multi-level organisational hierarchy which bears much of the responsibility for generating investment cycles; made prices much more realistic (even if they are not real market prices but simulated ones on a 'what if' basis, with 'if' referring to the existence of competition on the domestic market), and introduced a uniform (although not equilibrating) exchange rate. But enterprises are not, even now, autonomous economic agents. The most important obstacle to really decentralized, market-oriented reforms was left untouched.

Even without a multilevel hierarchical structure, without (many) commands and (much) rationing, managers continue to be dependent upon those who nominate them, decide upon their remuneration, and may recall them from their posts as well as upon *nomenklatura* behind the bureaucrats. Since within the existing framework it is loyalty that matters most, appointed managers are primarily evaluated on the basis of their loyalty, i.e. on the basis of their fulfillment of commands related to planned output targets, *ad hoc* commands, 'guiding principles', etc. rather than on the basis of efficiency as expressed by the bottom line effects of enterprise activities.

From 1968 to these days commands have usually taken the form of 'suggestions' but under the circumstances they are no less mandatory. With their present bonuses and, ultimately, the security of their position dependent upon their direct and indirect superiors (i.e. *nomenklatura* members), managers suffer from Dr. Jekyll and Mr. Hyde syndrome. They analyze in turn their possible options in terms of efficiency and then turn to various conflicting ' guiding principles ', some partial goals (like, e.g. energy saving, exporting for hard currency, etc.), as well as to enterprise-specific suggestions. If there are conflicts between the requirements of efficiency and those of loyalty (as understood in the system), the latter generally prevail. If following 'guiding principles', fulfilling partial targets and/or following suggestions turns out to be costly from the bottom line point of view, then their loyalty is rewarded through the 'soft' budget constraint. Enterprises obtain subsidies in one form or another (outright grants, low-interest credits that are later often cancelled, reduced taxes, etc.). Thus financial targets are fulfilled and managers may obtain their bonuses, well deserved by loyal behaviour (more on the issue, see Winiecki, 1986d).

Obviously, in Hungary the market has not been substituted for the traditional central planning and the institutional and procedural void has been filled by many auxiliary and guiding indicators (generally in conflict with one another), by bargaining *ex ante* between managers and their superiors for the expected values of these indicators, by participation of economic bureaucrats and party apparatchiks in the preparation of allegedly ' autonomous ' plans of enterprises, as well as by an amalgam of disguised and undisguised, formal and informal, persistent or *ad hoc* interventions in enterprise activities. Inevitable contradictions of such a process reinforced by the prevalent loyalty-based rather than efficiency-based choices sharply limited efficiency gains of Hungarian reforms. Consequently, patterns of economic growth, structural change and foreign trade have not been significantly better than those in other STEs (see, e.g. Bauer, 1984).

But the fact that the Hungarian economy is only a relative success would probably not deter those willing to emulate Hungarian reforms — for at least two reasons. First, the Hungarian reforms are a success relative to other STEs, and the ruling elites in the latter could count on some loosening of the natural resource constraint by reducing material intensity somewhat, as well as less severe disequilibrium, a better supplied consumer goods market and an appeased (or at least less discontented) population. Second, the Hungarian reforms would appeal to communist elites owing to their seemingly technocratic character — they do not reduce the traditional modes of control from above.

HUNGARIAN REFORMS — DIFFICULT TO EMULATE

There are, however, two reservations which cloud even a cautiously optimistic picture of the possible success in emulating the Hungarian reforms. The first is the questionable validity of the claim that the reforms are purely technocratic in character. The outstanding aspect of Hungarian economic performance is agriculture: equilibrium on the domestic food market, large export surpluses, quite high productivity, flexibility of producers. But Hungarian cooperatives not only obtained the right to choose their production profile (in and outside agriculture), but they also achieved a high degree of self-management, including the right to elect their managers. Thus not only has the organisational hierarchy been abolished, but also a large measure of participation in decision making was gained by the employees.

This latter did not survive intact the 'counterreformation' period when orthodoxy gained the upper hand. A requirement of party acceptance of managerial candidates before elections was reintroduced. This weakened workers' motivation, resulting over time in increased costs, as less care had to be compensated by more agricultural inputs. The best agricultural performance by co-operatives was in the late 1960s - early 1970s period. Since then private plots (of farmers, members of cooperatives, and towns-people) have been providing a rising proportion of total agricultural production.

Where there was no significant degree of participation, as in industry, the effects were not impressive. Probably as important as reforms in industry *per se* was the general atmosphere of cautious relaxation. This included an effort by the Hungarian leadership to depoliticise everyday life, making Hungarians forget about one of the most repellent aspects of the system. It was certainly a conces-sion on the part of the communist ruling elite, but it paid hand-somely in terms of better workers' morale and greater social stability.

Thus it is doubtful how much even the unimpressive improve-ments achieved outside agriculture owe to economic reforms. It should also be noted that in the 1961-80 period Hungary was the only STE in which the growth rate of consumer goods was higher than that of producers goods during each five-year plan (while the opposite was the case in all the other STEs). This was so *before, during and after* the introduction of the 1968 reforms. One may hypothesise that it was rather the ruling elite's collective memory of the year 1956, when communists, for once, found themselves, albeit briefly, on the receiving end of repression, that made them later more cautious in undertaking 'taut', 'mobilising', welfare-reducing, plans, as well as in avoiding other drastic excesses of arrogant extravaganza. In other words, they learned the lesson that if there is an outbreak of discontent Soviet assistance may come in time to save the system, but not necessarily to save them personally. The experience of Hungarian communists is unique in Eastern Europe and without this moderation attempts to emulate Hungary may fail.

Thus the replication of the Hungarian economic reforms, minus the Hungarian ruling elite's unique experience and minus its limited political concessions to society, would not bring even those relative successes that are the lure of this particular scenario. Moreover, Hungarian economic reforms are clearly an unfinished business and, without meeting some important political require-ments, may be not only unfinished but unfinishable. Clouds over the horizon are already visible in Hungary itself and they are not absent elsewhere. Thus if one adds to the above both less time and a less conducive environment for trial-and-error policies one may be justifiably doubtful about the effects of attempts to solve problems of strategies and decline of Soviet-type economies through the emulation of the Hungarian economic reforms.

ALTERNATIVE TWO: NECESSARY POLITICAL INPUTS TO ASSURE SUCCESS OF ECONOMIC REFORMS

We have so far looked at probable scenarios of economic change for East European STEs without reference to the third and most important determinant of the choice of remedial action, namely the interests of the ruling elites in maintaining the *status quo*. Awareness of the deteriorating performance and of alternative solutions is a necessary but not a sufficient condition for selection of a possible solution. It is the various interests involved, economic and non-economic, that narrow the list of possible solutions down to a few (if any) desirable ones. Any analysis of the interests of various groups of democracies would have to be much wider in scope, encompassing, among others, political parties, trade unions, business organisations and professional associations. Here, I shall limit myself to those organised groups which, taken together, constitute the four pillars of the communist system of government. As the political and economic components of the system are all but inseparable, far-reaching reforms in the economic area strongly affect the interests of all these groups. But are the pillars of the system, or even their top echelons, which make up the elite, as monolithic as sometimes portrayed? Are their interests identical? And, in consequence, would they all go to the same (extreme) extent in defending the *status quo*?

DIFFERENT INTERESTS OF SYSTEM-SUPPORTING GROUPS

The issues have not received the attention they merited in the analysis of possible solutions to the stagnation and decline of STEs. It is obvious that, given their limited or non-existent legitimacy, the pillars of the system prefer the *status quo* that gives them more than they could have obtained under the democratic alternative. But this does not mean that all those pillars of support -- the communist party apparatchiks, the bureaucrats from the multi-level management hierarchies, the police and the military -- would have the same interest in maintaining the political *status quo* if important political changes were necessary to reverse the deterioration of economic performance that is threatening to decrease (or is already decreasing) the economic benefits those groups derive from their dominant political position.

The participation of these four groups in power sharing has been extensively researched, but little attention has been devoted to their role in wealth sharing. It is the latter, however, that in my opinion is the key to understanding their potentially divergent attitudes to economic reforms coupled with political change that would be able to reverse the decline.

Let us put the question of wealth sharing in the communist system in a more systematic, and comparative, perspective. First of all, two modes of benefiting from the dominant position in the political system ought to be distinguished. One is a traditional, long recognized way of benefiting in non-democratic systems, that is through the appropriation of a larger share of the newly created wealth (national product) than would have been possible under the democratic alternative. In dictatorships the police and/or the military simply get better paid and enjoy more perquisites relative to the rest of society. Also, their professional needs (and desire for status symbols, like modern military equipment) have a priority claim on the state budget. The police and the military in the communist system do not differ much in this respect. The salaries may be relatively higher, the 'perks' may be relatively more important in terms of privileged access to goods in short supply, yet their *mode* of wealth sharing is much the same.

This cannot be said about the party apparatchiks and the bureaucracy, though. Traditional dictatorships do not know ruling parties of that sort. Nor do they know multi-level economic management hierarchies that spawn the ever-growing bureaucracies trying to manage STEs. These two pillars of the system may also help themselves to a larger slice of the economic pie, relative to the rest of society, but for them this is not the only, or even the most important, way of benefiting from the system. Political control of the economy, an important communist *credo*, allows those two groups to benefit not only by appropriating more of the newly created wealth, but also continuously to appropriate benefits by interfering in the process of wealth creation itself. It is the latter feature that sets the STEs apart from others.

There are two ways of benefiting from the system, over and above the way characteristic of 'ordinary' dictatorships. The first and most important is, of course, the *nomenklatura* system of party control over all important appointments, and especially enterprise managers. Party apparatchiks have traditionally taken advantage of this to appoint themselves and their cronies to well paid bureaucratic and managerial jobs. Once appointed, enterprise managers may (and do) return the favour by selling products in short supply directly to their colleagues in the party apparatus and/or selling them at discount prices, using phony excuses of lower quality (lower quality goods do reach the market, but those that are a form of kickback are carefully selected!). Managers themselves, their families and friends, benefit handsomely in a similar way.

If and when the modes of participation in wealth sharing are systematized in this manner, the differences between the party apparatchiks and the bureaucracy on the one hand and the police and the military on the other become clearer. Both subsets prefer the *status quo* to the democ_atic alternative because shared power permits them to draw bigger economic benefits than would have been possible otherwise. However, only the latter subset, party apparatchiks and the economic bureaucracy, are interested in the *mode* in which wealth is created. This explains why economic reforms fail in a communist system, or at least why they do not go far enough to make a decisive impact (in the Hungarian case). For their success depends on the two pillars of the system that stand to loose most from successful reforms!

There exists no theory of reforming a centrally planned economy but, in a nutshell, it may be said that such an economy shows greater distortions than other economies and, in consequence, reforms have to remove, or substantially reduce, distortions in three broad areas: the institutional setting, product and factor prices, and external linkages. In my opinion the removal of institutional distortions should precede everything else for it is the middle levels of the organizational hierarchy, whose jobs are threatened with extinction (industrial branch ministries, associations of enterprises), that offer the strongest resistance to reforms. Any serious reform has to make them superfluous and, if the hierarchy is left intact, that part of the economic bureaucracy concentrates on throwing sand into the machinery of reforms.

In this they are supported by the rest of the bureaucracy and by the party apparatchiks who tend to lose not so much their relatively well paid jobs, but the economic benefits they derive from interfering in the process of wealth creation. The more indirect policy measures supersede direct commands and the more autonomy enterprises possess in reacting to parameters (interest rates, exchange rates etc.), the less time and effort managers would be willing to spend on 'kickback' activities. Also, the more far-reaching the reforms are, the clearer it becomes that enterprise managers cannot be appointed by bureaucrats from above (and the party apparatchiks behind them), if they are not to be less interested in efficiency than in the whims and wishes of their superiors and the appartchiks who control appointments through the *nomenklatura* system. This is why two aspects of economic reforms, self-management (which would hold managers accountable for kickbacks) and appointment of managers on the basis of merit, with the abolition of the *nomenklatura* system (which would end the reservation of lucrative managerial positions for the dominant minority), have hitherto been successfully resisted. Actually, those who benefit economically from the system in a totalitarian rather than authoritarian way would resist changes in other areas as well. They would, for instance, be hostile to price reforms, because equilibrium prices would tend to reduce their welfare. In a shortage economy privileged access to otherwise rationed goods is a source of welfare gains, either in the form of a higher level of consumption than would be possible at equilibrium prices or in the form of higher income if goods acquired at below equilibrium prices are resold later at equilibrium (i.e. black market) ones. When, for example, car prices in Poland are equal to about 40% of the equilibrium price the gains from privileged buying are indeed significant. The same goes for other goods in short supply.[21] Thus it is obvious that the apparatchiks and the economic bureaucracy have more to lose because they benefit economically from the existing system both in the traditional way (in this way they do not differ from the police and the military) and in a non-traditional system-specific way (particularly through the *nomenklatura* system). They can therefore be expected to resist change in the economic component of the system more strongly.

MILITARY (POLICE) REGIME

This distinction may not have meant much in a period when, in spite of the waste of resources, production and — at a lower rate — consumption were still growing. But with production increasing slowly or stagnating and consumption stagnating or falling the situation may become different. With less to gain from the petrification of an economic system increasingly unable to cope with the problems of modern industrial society, and more to lose because of the shrinking of their own wealth (in absolute terms), the other two pillars of the system may come into conflict with the party and the bureaucracy. Judged in terms of successful economic reforms, the advantages of a scenario in which the communist party is pushed into the background, reduced to a largely ornamental role or dissolved altogether, and the military, with or without the police, take over the leading role in the country are considerable. The latter groups are not so attached to the model of central planning because they do not draw totalitarian material benefits from it. Consequently, they could be willing to discard it when returns to the system began to diminish or become negative.[22]

Almost as important in the success of economic reforms would be the elimination of the obnoxious politicisation of everyday life. The foundations of a military (or a military-police) regime would be those of an 'ordinary' rather than a totalitarian dictatorship and they would need neither Byzantine symbolic politics nor an unceasing barrage of mendacious propaganda to create a quasi-legitimacy for themselves. In other words the system would then rely on authoritarian 'don'ts', rather than on totalitarian 'do's'. The economy could then be freed from many of the constraints analysed above, while society, assured of the opportunity to realise its aspirations in the economic (even if not in the political) sphere and freed from a major irritant (politicization) could turn its energies to entrepreneurship, innovativeness, and simply better work, all of which would become more profitable.

The scenario need not stop at this point. It is obvious that, with the main obstacle to economic reforms neutralised or removed, the 'ordinary' dictatorship need not become a permanent feature of the political landscape. The example of Spain clearly shows that greater reliance on the market and the concomitant opening up of the economy to external influences result in both rapidly rising incomes and an incomparably more complex set of economic and non-economic domestic and transnational interactions. As a result, the ruling elite may find clinging to power both less important, owing to the increased level of wealth, and more costly, owing to the inordinate amount of effort necessary to control an open society dictatorially.

We return to this case later, since its lessons are important for yet another scenario. At this point I would like to add one rather obvious comment. In outlining the above scenario I have not differentiated between the Soviet Union and the smaller countries of Eastern Europe under Soviet influence. If this scenario of military (or military-police) dominance and shift to an 'ordinary' dictatorship were to take place in any of the latter countries, the new ruling elite would also take over from the respective communist party the role of guarantor of the Soviet Union's strategic interests in the country concerned.

It is worth noting that the martial law period gave rise to some speculation that Poland would become an early case of such a scenario, combining 'some decentralisation and marketisation with a degree of militarisation' and that the system would evolve toward that prevailing in Spain under Franco and similar regimes (see, e.g. Gomulka, 1982). Subsequent developments, however, have made the Polish case look more and more like the 'normalisation' of post-1968 Czechoslovakia. As there are no resources to support an increase in consumption to mitigate political repression, the failure of attempts to enforce such a scenario is certain and a new shock all but inevitable.

At times it looks as if the present communist leadership in Poland were in two minds as to which aim to pursue vacillating between the Czechoslovak-like 'normalization' and Hungarian 'goulash communism' but — for obvious reasons — without goulash.

One way or another, we still have to wait for the military type detotalitarianization-of-the-economy scenario to materialize.

SELF-LIMITATION BY PARTY

Yet another scenario that would have a reasonable chance of economic success, is self-limitation by the communist party itself. It ought to be stressed from the outset that its probability of success is markedly higher than the probability of its occurrence. I have explained why the communist party has the strongest interest in resisting any change in the traditional Soviet-type model and its political ramifications. But the scenario, even if not highly probable, is not impossible. Havrylyshyn, in the report to the Club of Rome on the roads leading towards more effective societies (Havrylyshyn, 1980), gives some pointers with respect to the USSR as to why the ruling communist parties might, after all, be interested in limiting their role both in the economy and in politics and putting the economy on a path of economic efficiency and growing wealth (rather than growing production that feeds upon itself). Beside the increased pressures stemming from economic decline, Havrylyshyn rightly underlines the increased costs of 'keeping the lid on' the population when the contradictions between theory and reality cannot be camouflaged much longer. Also, there is the cost of party dominance in managing an ever more complex system like the Soviet Union, which 'absorbs a disproportionate amount of energy, which could be used otherwise for production of useful economic and social goods and services' (Ibid., p.43).

This can best be explained in terms of Deutsch's distinction between gross and net power (Deutsch, 1966). Gross power is understood to be the amount of change imposed by the application of power, while net power is the amount of change that would have been accepted without the application of power. The greater the difference between gross and net power the greater the amount of effort and resources necessary to achieve certain ends (whether related to change or to maintaining the *status quo*). This difference is very great in the communist system. In economic terms it may be said that to achieve economic growth the difference between the total uses of resources (gross production) and the amount of new material wealth created (net material product) is strikingly higher than in MEs. One may assume, judging by the size of the respective party, economic control, police and propaganda apparatuses, that it is very costly in terms of human effort as well.

When the total wealth begins to decrease and so does the volume of benefits drawn by the ruling elite, the apportioning of a greater share of the shrinking pie to themselves to maintain their absolute level of welfare may be a short term solution. But it is one which is likely to boomerang, either in the form of falling production quality and quantity or open discontent. The late nineteenth century black educator, Booker T. Washington, stressed the futility of slavery by pointing to the amount of power that would have to be expended, saying that 'the only way the white man in the South can keep the Negro in the ditch is to stay in the ditch with him' (quoted in Deutsch, 1966, p.115). With falling living standards and ever more discontented societies, ruling elites may find it so effort-consuming to control the sullen or rebellious societies, while getting less and less in terms of their own welfare, that, after some time, they may find it convenient to enlarge the power base and gradually or radically relinquish the system-specific controls.

The withdrawal of the party from interference in the wealth creation process, as well as the dismantling of the petrified structure of central planning, is a key ingredient of success. The experience of Yugoslavia clearly shows that the dismantling of the latter by itself is not enough. Given its total political control, the Yugoslav communist party retains the ability to interfere in the selection of managers and to lean on regional and local administrations and banks, with the resultant strongly negative outcomes. Investment cycles in Yugoslavia have not followed the time pattern of STEs; the interaction between central planners and enterprises within the five-year planning framework has been absent in Yugoslavia. But cycles and over-investment have continued and non-viable 'political factories', products of interference, have been lavishly sprinkled all over the country. Efficiency has not been markedly higher than under central planning.

This is why the enlargement of the power base is a prerequisite of success in the economic area and not only a democratisation measure *per se.* It is the developing framework of checks and balances, constraining the freedom of party apparatchiks to interfere in and sponge on the economy, that would bring improvements in economic performance simply by removing some of the most serious system-specific causes of waste, corruption and uncertainty. The depoliticisation of everyday life would also contribute, as I stressed in the case of the previous scenario too, to a more relaxed environment for economic activity. Incentives for risk-taking, entrepreneurship, innovation and, simply, good work are not enough. The population also needs to be reasonably sure that the laws will not be changed overnight (and retroactively at that), that the fruits of their labour will not be taken away as a result and they themselves subjected to yet another vilification campaign, and, finally, that their pursuit of material and intellectual aims will be conducted in an atmosphere devoid of mendaciousness and the no less irritating necessity to go through the motions of symbolic politics.

Just like in the earlier scenario it is possible that, after initial successes in terms of economic performance, and resultant rising welfare, the system would continue to evolve in a democratic direction. After all, as history has proved, there is in the long run a very strong positive correlation between democracy and high living standards. As Havrylyshyn rightly points out, two countries which previously nourished imperial ambitions, Germany and Japan, turned their great energies inward, after military defeat and built very efficient, prosperous economies and democratic, politically free societies. In the case of the USSR the decline of the extremely wasteful and increasingly inefficient economy may create as great a therapeutic shock as the military defeat was to Germany and Japan. These considerations apply to an even greater extent to the smaller East European countries which have no superpower ambitions and feel the system-specific constraints even more strongly.

I.5 IN PLACE OF CONCLUSIONS

There is not much new that can be added. Conclusions concerning both the present deterioration and the future prospects of STEs, as well as their determinants, are to be found throughout the pages, and summarising them now would be both uninteresting and superfluous. In consequence, I will add only four brief remarks constituting comments on my earlier discussion.

First, the outlook for Eastern Europe is gloomy. Even if one takes into account differences in economic performance between countries, the system-specific causes of stagnation and decline show rather clearly what would come next. The picture is even more depressing because of the clear recognition that the system of central planning has been unable to cope with problems that have long ago been solved by the market system.   STEs are not yet anywhere near the economic, social, psychological and other problems MEs are coping with at their higher levels of development. Nor will they reach such levels, given their inability to solve problems, the elimination of which is absolutely crucial, if those higher levels are ever to be attained.

Second, it is not surprising that the only scenarios that offer a reasonable chance of success are those envisaging the transformation of the whole communist system, not only of its economic component. Without such a transformation the lasting reversal of the long-term deterioration is clearly impossible. The Hungarian scenario may improve the situation slightly and temporarily, the West German 'umbrella' may make the strain in the GDR economy somewhat less visible (and less painful for the 'other' Germans), the plentiful resources of the Soviet Union may permit the elite to prolong yesterday a little longer — but none of these is much more than a temporary reprieve.

Third, I have discussed the STEs of Eastern Europe. That does not mean, however, that economies in other parts of the world, that opted for central planning economically and resembled East European countries in their political arrangements have fared any better. Elsewhere I have analysed (see, Winiecki, 1984e), the performance in the 1970s of a group of developing countries (LDCs) that chose to a smaller or larger extent the Soviet path to development, and compared it with the average growth performance of low income and middle income LDCs and, particularly, with the group of newly industrializing countries (NICs) that chose the opposite path, namely greater marketization and export orientation of their economies. The results were highly significant. The growth rate of a group of 9 countries that chose central planning as a dominant form of organization and for which the data were available was 1% annually (unweighted), with big variations between countries, compared with 3% for all low income and 5.1% for all middle income LDCs and 8.9% annually (unweighted) for Asian NICs. In the last group variations between countries were much smaller.

No less significantly, on a case-by-case basis, a regime change in an LDC toward greater centralization of economic management resulted in a marked fall in economic growth rate, while the reverse change toward greater market orientation resulted in acceleration of the growth rate. Angola, Ethiopia, Mozambique, Madagascar, Peru and Jamaica all experienced a drop in growth rate after their regime changed, if the 1970s are compared with the 1960s, while the opposite was the case with Egypt, Indonesia, Somalia and the Sudan,[23] where growth accelerated in the 1970s in spite of the more difficult international economic environment. Evidently the decline is system-wide and not confined to Eastern Europe.

Fourth, and last, the decline is not confined to economics and narrowly interpreted living standards, i.e. current consumption. The scars of pollution are much uglier and pollution itself greater when generated by the 'civilization of poverty and stupidity' as a Cracow columnist wrote about Poland's environmental degradation. This view can be easily extended to other STEs where the same problems are created by the same system-specific features. Also, a combination of high socio-psychological pressure upon those living under totalitarianism, bad working conditions, the above-mentioned pollution and unhealthy food due to unsanitary conditions has resulted in what another, better known columnist,

Alain Besançon, aptly called the return of death (*L'Express*, 1985, September 6). Various demographic time series began to reverse themselves in STEs (with the Soviet Union in the lead) showing increasing mortality and decreasing life expectancy.

All walks of life tend to coalesce to paint a bleaker future than the one derived from economic analysis only. No surprise then that many people shudder at the thought of what the future holds should the system remain basically the same. Fortunately for East European societies, the system's ability to survive intact is weakening fast and this may be the only ray of hope in the otherwise discouraging picture outlined in this part of the book.

Part II
The West

II.1. INTRODUCTORY REMARKS

With the economic trends and prospects of totalitarianist collectivism (that is, to put it simply, extreme collectivism) still fresh in mind, it is not to the turbulent 1970s, nor specifically to the oil price explosions, that I want to draw readers' attention. Much more important for the trends and prospects of the West, in my view, are the issues related to the impact of post-war trends upon the efficiency of the capitalist private enterprise-based market system.

For a variety of reasons the long period of unprecedented growth of wealth in the 1950s and 1960s reduced our understanding of its real sources. The wealth came to be regarded as something akin to *manna-falling-from-Heaven* rather than the effect of purposeful efforts made in the efficiency-promoting environment of the market system. The great wave of irrationalism that swept through Western societies and, to some extent, the body politic at the end of the 1960s and the beginning of the 1970s also contributed to the deteriorating flexibility. With its foundations weakened, the market system responded to the external shocks of the 1970s sluggishly and at a markedly higher cost in terms of unemployed production factors.

Since the weakening of the market system is an outcome of governmental policies pursuing various efficiency-impairing goals, as well as adverse effects of other (allegedly efficiency-neutral) policies, they are remediable first of all by the democratic political process. At the sub-national level, the various redistributive coalitions — to use Mancur Olson's phrase (1980) — are also best controlled in the same way, both directly, through legal restraint, and indirectly, through measures to strengthen competition.

It is, thus, a political will not only to pursue important social goals in a way that minimizes adverse effects on efficiency but also to redress damage inflicted on the market system so that it could function (reasonably) efficiently that has long been the necessary basis of change for the better. The adjective 'reasonably' has been inserted above in acknowledgement of the fact that efficiency is not an end in itself. However, any increase in wealth is predicated in the contemporary world upon increases in efficiency and if important social goals include a further increase in wealth — which seems to be the case — the efficiency properties of the *market system* should be maintained and — where necessary — restored.

Also, if important social goals include political democracy based upon individualist liberal values — which recently seems to have been increasingly the case — the efficiency properties of the *capitalist private enterprise-based market system* should be carefully nurtured. There is in the longer term a perfect positive correlation between wealth, the capitalist private enterprise-based market system, and political democracy. My hope is that the first part of this book has underlined the importance of the market system and political democracy for wealth creation in the sense that — in their absence — the wealth generated is pitifully small in spite of the incomparably larger amount of resources employed by the Soviet-type collectivist states in their quest for it.

As the 1980s progressed, the political will to improve the efficiency of the market system became visible throughout the Western world — a well appreciated fact. What has been somewhat less well appreciated is that, for the first time since the industrial revolution, both economic and technological change are working *for*, not against, the efficient functioning of this system. There are also lasting political implications of economic and technological change, contributing to the resurgence of both the market orientation and the accompanying individualist liberal values.

In our discussion of possible scenarios later we shall take cognizance of these interactions between economics and technology and politics. How quickly the capitalist private enterprise-based market-oriented liberal order re-establishes itself will depend on the amount of resistance to change put up by protagonists of the decreasingly appealing etatist alternative and the collectivist egalitarianist vision which in some respects is still more appealing to many.

It may also depend on the way the resurgent market-based individualist order is able to integrate the satisfaction of needs for what have become known as public goods, as well as for an income safety net, into its fundamentally competitive framework. But since old beliefs (even if discredited) die hard and since there are important vested interests involved in pursuing their vision, we also consider the possible consequences of a return to the collectivist and etatist trend.

II.2. DECLINING EFFICIENCY OF THE MARKET SYSTEM: CAUSES AND EFFECTS

Much has been written since the late 1970s about *growing rigidities in factor markets*, as well as other effects of the visible hand of government on the efficiency of the market system, the dearth of risk-bearing, etc. Issues have not only been studied in increasing detail but conclusions stemming from them have been persuasively presented in defence of the impaired market system (see, e.g. Balassa, Giersch, Kindleberger, Lindbeck, Lundberg, Lord McFadzean, Walbroeck to mention but a few). Adding to their penetrative criticism would be both superfluous and difficult. Consequently, what follows is not a systematic and balanced (even if sketchy) survey but some highly selective reflections from another vantage point, from which certain issues seem to weigh more heavily upon the efficiency of the market system than has usually been assumed by critics of the post-war etatist and collectivist trends in the West. If certain causes or symptoms are omitted or barely mentioned, it is not intended to imply that they are unimportant or even less important. It simply means that there is no divergence in these respects between the weights usually ascribed to their importance and the weights ascribed by the present writer.

Thus, there is no divergence in the critical assessment of the activity of redistributive coalitions and/or governments that resulted in a rise in the real wage of labour 10% greater than in GDP *per capita* during the 1970s — and that at a time of massive outflow of wealth to oil-producing countries. But I would like to draw attention to some other sources of such redistributive reflexes in the face of radically changed circumstances, which have not usually been emphasised in the way that growing failure to understand the real sources of wealth creation on the part of large segments of the population, monopoly power of trade unions and complacency of governments sure of their Keynesian remedies have been.

EXPANSION BASED ON BIGNESS

On a more complex plane, the expansion of the 1950s and 1960s created a distorted image of the sources of affluence. It was expansion based, in the main, on bigness. When each doubling of productive capacity brought about, applying a rule of thumb, about a 30% productivity increase, affluence seemed to appear as a *Deus from an ever bigger machina*. Not much entrepreneurship or innovation seemed to be necessary to build ever bigger plants. Increased concentration, in turn, further weakened the individual worker's perception of linkages between his own efforts and the effects in the form of his rising affluence. Entrepreneurs seemed to be giving way to managers of planned expansion.

The apparently shrinking role of entrepreneurship and risk-bearing in general intensified negative attitudes towards profits, and distributed profits in particular, attitudes carefully nurtured by a barrage of socialist/populist propaganda. The resultant misperceptions of both the role and the real level of profits have been a continuing obstacle to a more balanced distribution of productivity gains.[24]

Moreover, not only wage levels but also wage differentials became distorted in the process. Given a type of technical progress consisting mainly of process improvement and a more general 'the bigger, the better' philosophy, the highest wage increases were often accorded not to those whose skills were the scarcest, or to the most skilled, or those working under the most exacting conditions, but to those possessing the strongest bargaining power. Inevitably, the 'big battalions' did best, pushing wages in industries with economies of scale out of line with wage increases elsewhere. (The U.S. motor industry, where a semi-skilled operative could earn about twice as much per hour as a skilled car mechanic in a repair shop, is but one — if telling — example of these distortions.)

Not only did inter-industry relative wages become distorted but occupational differences also narrowed markedly. The process went further in the Scandinavian countries than elsewhere, but it continued in Western Europe until this decade. With highly educated specialists expecting their discounted lifetime income to be only 10-50% higher than that of low-skilled blue collar workers, strong disincentives to strenuous effort on the job by the former were certainly created (data for Sweden, taken from Lindbeck, 1981a).[25]

Distorted wage levels and relative wages are but a few symptoms of a litany of causes contributing to the declining flexibility of the labour market. These, however, have been eloquently formulated elsewhere (see, in particular, Lindbeck, 1981b, and the literature quoted therein). So have other, related, issues of the shifting of attention from wealth creation to tax avoidance and other socially unproductive but personally rewarding activities (including illegal ones). Disincentives to save and, more generally, the declining efficiency of capital markets will not be analyzed here as on these points my views and emphasis are in agreement with earlier critics.

GOVERNMENT vs. MARKET FAILURE

Although much has been learned since the time of Pigou about 'market failure' and corrective measures, understanding of the cost of alternative measures, including governmental intervention, has only recently become more fully appreciated. Public choice analysts have now offered a theory of 'government failure' which rejects the 'market failure' theory's claim of costless government intervention. This sober analysis has undermined the socialist mystique that the state and 'politics' somehow work towards some transcendent 'public good' (Buchanan, 1979). But again much has been written about *the (costly) visible hand of government* trying to redress some real or imaginary market failures or achieve ever more profuse goals affecting both the body economic and the body social. Therefore only one, somewhat less well perceived, aspect of this very extensive issue will be examined now, namely th. ....pact of 'the bigger, the better' attitudes upon industrial policies. In the 1960s West European governments often pressed private enterprises to merge to create what in France were called 'national champions', which were supposedly to be better equipped to compete with large American companies. However, by altering the market structure, governments sometimes weakened rather than strengthened the ability of West European enterprises to perform. For it was not, or not only, the scale of economic activity and associated advantages but the competition on the large American market that made U.S. enterprises more efficient. This lesson has, by the way, been learned by the Japanese, whose much misunderstood[26] and over-emphasized industrial policies have always fostered competition. Thus, while many national champions continue to rely on often small national markets for the bulk of their sales and profits, and even then often need a dose of governmental support, Japanese companies, aggressively competing with local enterprises and among themselves, rapidly increase their share of foreign sales and profits.

It is also ironic that the call to bigness became most strongly articulated (see, e.g. Servan-Schreiber, 1968) exactly at the time when diseconomies of scale began to appear in highly concentrated industries and the role of growth engine began to shift towards industries based on entrepreneurship and innovation. With the advent of the turbulent 1970s, and a more or less permanent reduction in demand for the products of industries based on economies of scale, compounded by the increasing competition from third countries, industrial policies shifted towards propping up the declining industries. Most of the money went to big enterprises, and more specifically to the worst performers among them. Given their size and resultant political clout, they were able to gather enough support to survive — at the cost of others. This policy of robbing Peter to pay Paul brought about a general decline in economic efficiency because it was the reverse of the type of structural change that results in the most significant productivity gains, i.e. when more efficient firms expand relative to less efficient ones.

CREATIVE DESTRUCTION

The end of this 'the bigger, the better' era, with its perception of economic growth as the management of planned expansion, revived interest in the Schumpeterian notion of 'creative destruction', according to which the economy is characterized by accelerating or decelerating — but nonetheless continuing — structural change. Consequently, the birth, expansion, maturing, contraction and death of firms and industries are natural and healthy characteristics of the market system. Phasing out is then necessary to make room for more efficient and innovative producers, and the associated dislocations should be made less painful not by continuous and increasingly costly propping up of contracting firms and industries but by creating a more encouraging environment for the expanding and new ones, including increased occupational and geographic mobility of labour (especially but not exclusively redundant labour).

This revival coincided with the shift of the role of growth engine from industries based on economies of scale to industries based on entrepreneurship and innovation and with more keenly perceived *disincentives to entrepreneurship and risk-bearing in general.* As stressed in the literature, it was the distortions in the factor markets (first and foremost the disincentives resulting from high marginal tax rates and especially severe taxation of capital gains), the maze of governmental regulation, as well as the generally hostile political climate that caused the dearth of private entrepreneurs and — in a wider sense — of entrepreneurial behaviour. Here too a large part of the explanations linking causes, symptoms and effects have become well established in the last 5-10 years. These explanations also received strong support from the property rights theorists and their followers among the 'new economic historians' led by the late Douglass North. We shall therefore concentrate primarily on some underexplored linkages with bigness and some misunderstanding surrounding Schumpeter's view of the forces driving the entrepreneur.

It should be stressed that the pattern of economic growth dominant in the 1950s and 1960s contributed to the problem in question. The disdainful views long held by some eminent left-leaning economists about the negligible contribution of entrepreneurs to wealth creation (see, e.g. Kaldor, 1934, and Joan Robinson, 1934) seemed to find practical confirmation in 'the bigger, the better' era. Such thinking affected not only owner-entrepreneurs but inventive employers as well. Invention in the era of large firms was conceived to be a product of large scale R and D effort; the individual inventor, whether insider or outsider, was a thing of the past. Concentration was about as much as many on the left understood from Schumpeter until the 1980s (on this point, see the witty article by Alain Leroux, 1986).

SCHUMPETERIAN MISUNDERSTANDINGS

But unfortunately it was not only the collectivist left that misunderstood Schumpeter. Many analysts regarded as Schumpeterian the view that entrepreneurs generally and innovators particularly seek success for its own sake, without regard for material rewards. Properly rewarded or not, they would continue to bear risk, be creative, etc. However, on careful reading of Schumpeter, three goals of the entrepreneur, beside the joy of creation, can be distinguished: (1) obtaining high material reward, (2) building a monument of success to oneself (a successful, innovative firm); and (3) founding an empire (leaving that firm to one's heirs). If we look at these three goals it is not difficult to see why post-war entrepreneurship tended to become stifled over time. High marginal taxes reduced the chances of achieving the first goal, extensive government regulations acted as a constraint on achieving the second, and high inheritance taxes made the third even more difficult. In an environment where all three constraints were strong, entrepreneurship suffered and wealth creation fell significantly below the potential level.

Such underutilization might occur in various ways. Potential entrepreneurs might decide that so poorly rewarded activity was simply not worth pursuing and remain in employment, where the risk/reward trade-off was more advantageous, given the environment for entrepreneurship. Those already owning and managing firms might pursue opportunities less aggressively, play safe by choosing options that brought smaller but more predictable returns, or decide not to expand above a certain threshold, beyond which the nuisance of regulation and trade union pressures increase exponentially. (Italy is probably the best example of the third option on a mass scale, but evidence of it has been visible for some years in other Western countries as well.)

Futhermore, innovativeness has not only been thwarted but also distorted, for reasons related partly to the growing size of enterprises. Large firms tend to be more bureaucratic in general and less prone to risk bearing. In my opinion, the combined effect of playing by the rule book and playing safe was a change in the balance between product innovation and process innovation in favour of the latter. For it is much more difficult to convince the unimaginative bureaucrats of a large firm of the possible higher profits from a proposed new product that is still only an idea than it is to convince them of the lower costs of a new technological process. In such an organizational environment incremental improvements are much more easily accepted than novelties, tinkering rather than radical change. At least a portion of the complaints heard for years about the lack of a sufficient number of new products that could become growth engines for advanced Western economies has its source in these developments.

CONSTRAINTS ON ENTREPRENEURSHIP

In smaller, more trade-dependent economies the combined impact of high levels of taxation and regulatory constraints on entrepreneurship[27] may have resulted in a marked decline in the establishment and successful expansion of new private firms in industry and competitive, i.e. exportable, services. Potential entrepreneurs would be deterred by the insufficiency of their own savings in the high-tax environment, as well as by the absence of private venture capital in the environment that penalizes high risk/high profit activities through especially severe capital gains taxes. Competitive position would then increasingly depend on the established large private firms, whose bigness gave them a stronger bargaining position in resisting or moderating efficiency-reducing governmental intrusions.[28]

These firms, however, are less innovative and flexible in their reactions to changing world demand. The large shifts in demand structure over the last 10-15 years weakened many of them considerably. With large established firms in some industries disappearing or living off government subsidies and new ones not replacing them as foreign exchange earners, the decline of highly taxing and highly interventionist but at the same time highly trade-dependent countries may only be a matter of time. Nonetheless the rate of formation, survival and expansion of new firms, including their foreign trade role, has rarely been studied, still less stimulated.

To sum up, with less efficiently functioning markets, declining willingness to bear risk, and more and more extensive, contradictory, and uncertainty-increasing governmental regulation, the allocative ability of market economies — the very foundation of their outstanding performance — has been impaired. A particularly strong impact on their performance is attributable to various effects of egalitarianism-inspired tax systems and wage pressures that reduced, often drastically, income differentials — yet another foundation of the performance-rewarding market system.

The rigidities injected into the system have not only had increasingly harmful, wealth reducing, effects: these effects have also included a shift away from the observable economy. In all Western countries resistance to excessive taxation that reduced the link between performance and reward below the acceptable level gave rise to a range of tax avoidance activities, both legal and illegal (market or non-market, monetary or barter type). The feeling of injustice[29] runs deep and across the whole social spectrum (surprisingly, perhaps, for avowed egalitarians!). The resultant "invisible", "submerged", "unobserved", "underground" or "black" economies are variously estimated as ranging from 5% to as much as 30% of GNP. Even in societies known for their cohesion and the generally cooperative behaviour of their members, such as Sweden, the total value of unobserved transactions is estimated as being within the 5-20% range (IUI *Yearbook*, 1982-1983).

ENVIRONMENT HOSTILE TO MARKETS

The adverse changes analyzed or briefly indicated above could not have continued for so long if it had not been for *the hostile socio-political environment for the capitalist, private enterprise-based market system*. With the crisis of the 1930s fresh in mind and the new Keynesian prescription so appealing (while its cost surfaced only very slowly), belief in the market system was less than complete to say the least. Calls for a strong visible government hand to correct real or imaginary market failures, for government planning, as well as for other purposeful intrusions into the functioning of markets were very loud in the 1950s and early 1960s. They came not only from the collectivist left but often from those who thought them to be efficiency-increasing measures and, consequently, the best defense against the totalitarianist version of collectivism.

The voices of those like Hayek who warned against the efficiency illusion of collectivist planning were barely heard in the intellectual community. Even some classical liberals succumbed to that illusion and argued, like Wilhelm Roepke, that the capitalist private enterprise-based market system should be retained even if it were able to provide less material wellbeing than centrally planned collectivism because it alone was able to maintain the freedom of the individual which was so indispensable for spiritual wellbeing. His pessimistic views about the efficiency of the market system made a profound impact upon this author in his student years and led him for a long time to accept a much greater degree of governmental intrusion into the market system than he now regards as desirable for the system's efficiency. But this is a personal aside only.

The environment for the market system as it existed in the West — particularly in Western Europe — could not have been propitious under the above circumstances. Even the somewhat weaker economic growth of the United States *vis-à-vis* Western Europe in the period in question was ascribed to the lower degree of governmental intervention, for instance in the influential book by Andrew Shonfield (1965).[30] With the technological trends seemingly supporting the concept of managing planned expansion by ever bigger enterprises, the ultimate dependence of the unprecedented prosperity in the West on market sources remained obscured.

I have tried to examine certain phenomena as they appeared to large segments of contemporary Western societies, and their impact upon the environment for the market system. It should be stressed that certain developments might have made the efficient functioning of the market system *look* somewhat less indispensable for material wellbeing. What happened at the end of the 1960s and the early 1970s, however, did not even *appear* substantiated.

The wave of irrationalism that swept through the Western body social and politic turned a rather unfriendly environment for the capitalist, private enterprise-based market system into a really hostile one. Even Western democracy came under attack. The interdependence between the two was all but forgotton in many segments of Western societies and their elites. Curious double standards evolved. On the theoretical plane, the existing market system and Western democracy were compared with pure (and often pure nonsense!) ideal alternatives and invariably found wanting. At the same time the existing totalitarian systems, as well as ugly Third World dictatorships, with systemic features so disquietingly similar to the proposed alternatives, were conveniently forgotten in these biased comparisons.

On the practical, comparative systems plane *real* features of the market system were compared with the *professed* features of the socialist system or, given the Soviet-Chinese split, the socialist systems. Deeds were evaluated against words. Ignorance about the features of the Soviet-type system, reinforced by readiness to accept anything un-Western by giving it the benefit of the doubt, affected almost all segments of the elite. On the far left of the intellectual spectrum Johann Galtung — who was then turning out a new leftist utopia once a month — proclaimed triumphantly in every discussion on any social or economic issue that "as usual, the Chinese (meaning: Maoists) have the answer".

But people who would probably feel offended at being called not even leftist but just left-leaning also spread similarly unsubstantiated nonsense. Thomas Kimball, a prominent American conservationist, for example, after touring the USSR under the careful guidance of his hosts expressed the conviction that 'when the Soviet leadership really wants to protect the environment, it can do it with an order, a stroke of the pen, a new law. It is almost that simple compared with the process of getting our many divergent forces together from Congress, to private industry, to citizens' groups' (1973, p. 10). This praise for authoritarianist solutions uttered without understanding of the role of law in the Soviet system, without knowing how the preferences of the ruling group affect the fulfillment of specific commands and general rules, without acknowledging the impact of these preferences upon the attitudes towards the environment at various levels of the economic bureaucracy, was typical of well meaning but ill-informed propagandists of undemocratic solutions among Western intellectual elites.

No more than a decade after the peak period of unreason we heard that communist China had lost most of the time in pursuit of a coercive utopia that brought the Chinese people little but suffering and a subsistence level living standard — and that from the highest functionaries of the ruling group. In about the same time span it transpired that Eastern Europe is the most polluted part of the world, that East Germany emits more than four times as much sulphur dioxide *per capita* as the Federal Republic (and at half the living standard at that!) and that forests in Siberia are being felled or burned by neglect at a conbined rate of 1.2 million hectares *per annum* while reforestation proceeds at only one-sixth of that rate. The data are new but the basis of similar assessments was already available then; it was simply brushed aside in the hectic, unhealthy search for the un-Western.

A thriving 'blame industry' developed at the time, to use the apt term coined by Jean-Francois Revel (1984). Many liberal intellectuals joined it as a way of "redemption" for the real or imaginary sins of the Western economic and/or political system. For some strange reason they forgot that it was this system that had allowed them to become what they were, that is independent individuals in democratic, affluent societies, pursuing their intellectual aims free from state directives in their respective areas of interest. Less surprising was participation in the ' blame industry ' by those new leftists of a totalitarian inclination for whom the very fact that intellectuals, or whoever, could pursue anything free from collectivist directives, however labelled (e.g. 'people's will'), was anathema.

With a thriving 'blame industry' , appreciation of the fact that constraints upon or shrinking numbers of autonomous centres of decision making in the private sector tilt the balance not only against the efficiency of the market system but, in the longer run, against Western democracy itself declined even further (on this point see, e.g. Baechler, 1980).[31] Capitalism, profit, private ownership, market forces, etc., became almost dirty words. It is this hostile environment that bred a string of interventionist measures which not only constrained the performance of firms on increasingly distorted markets but pushed Western societies much further than before toward egalitarianism. And while the wave of irrationalism receded, egalitarianism — for complex reasons — registered continuing advances in the period between the two oil price jumps, further corroding the link between performance and reward upon which the market system is based.

II.3. SLOW AWAKENING AND PORTENTS OF CHANGE

Especially on the democratic left (communists and new leftists blamed 'capitalist exploitation' for everything, including excessive rainfall ...) it has been almost a ritual to blame the subsequent oil shocks for the economic slowdown, mounting unemployment, balooning budget deficits and high inflation. Only a minority, although a growing one, held a different view. To them the problems of the 1970s and the early 1980s were the outcome of long-term changes in Western economies and societies which would have taken place anyway, oil crisis or not. In other words they regarded them as caused by endogenous, domestic factors, in spite of the fact that they afflicted almost all Western economies. The consequences of the two oil shocks, including the wealth transfer to oil exporting countries, accelerated the inevitable developments, made them more painful and brought the rigidities imposed upon the market system into sharper focus. (This last outcome might have had a salutary effect in the final analysis as far as the West's future is concerned.) Thus, on the eve of the first oil shock, private enterprise, drained of its own resources by the wage explosion and higher taxes, short of external capital owing to the fall in savings, lacking entrepreneurship and willingness to bear risk because of the decreasing rewards and — last but not least — deprived of ideological support by the increasingly hostile criticism of the market system, stood weakened to such an extent that any deterioration in the general economic situation was bound to put serious strains on all Western economies.

The awakening from the collectivist and etatist dream proceeded at a slow pace, however. Both governments and unions, more often than not, repeated their previous behaviour. Governments increased their spending (and the size of the public sector) while trade unions continued to press for higher real wages in spite of faltering productivity and the economic slowdown. In some countries (e.g. France, Italy, Belgium) real wages of manual workers increased by about 20 percentage points more than GDP *per capita* in the 1971-1980 period. Given the generally low share of capital and of the self-employed in national income, it is obvious that these gains had to be made at the expense of their colleagues, or more accurately ex-colleagues, elsewhere i.e. those who became unemployed as a result, and pensioners. But these developments do not reveal the whole picture for they do not consider the other costs of the expansion of the public sector, the various forms of relief for lame duck private firms far exceeding the costs of mere wage increases[32], etc.

THREE IMPORTANT CHANGES

Three other developments made the economic impact of the oil shocks on the fundamentally weakened Western economies even stronger. *First*, all economies, but especially Western economies, have been undergoing accelerated structural change. Industries based on economies of scale, the core of rapid post-war growth, clearly began losing their dynamism. Large changes in the relative prices of energy and raw materials, on the one hand, further reduced a demand which was already growing at decreasing rates, while, on the other hand, they acted as a spur to technological change. The combined impact accelerated the medium to longer run fall in demand for metals, bulk chemicals (including synthetic materials), refinery products etc. Stagnating demand for these products has been a permanent feature of the West's economic growth pattern ever since.

Second, the open international trading system caused changes in comparative advantages in certain industries to be felt more strongly at precisely that time. For it was the turbulent 1970s that witnessed the rapid expansion of an increased range of manufactured exports from newly industrializing countries.

Both developments generated stronger pressures for support from vested interests in the affected industries. The resultant distortions grew bigger and structures became even less flexible in consequence. The costs of support were also great. By the end of the 1970s total subsidies in the EEC were equal to 2.4% of the GDP of the group. In some countries (e.g. Sweden, Belgium) they reached 4% and more. and this tells us nothing about the costs of not responding to changes in world demand in terms of both forgone output and employment.

Third, and last, value changes and demographic developments also magnified the macroeconomic problems affecting Western economies. Both the rapid rise in the participation rates of women and the temporary increase in young entrants to the labour market (an "echo" of the earlier baby boom) more or less coincided with the economic slowdown. Increased labour supply contributed to a significant extent to mounting unemployment.

As the 1970s progressed, strains began to appear everywhere. The uncontrollable rise in the cost of state intervention in the economy and of maintaining excessively ambitious welfare systems (based more on collectivist preferences than actual needs for protection) strained resources so much that it led to a more or less severe macroeconomic clamp-down. And this stuck, in spite of the strong protests and vocal opposition of those adversely affected by these changed policies. It is the persistent and in some countries continuously high inflation that indicates the resistance of various social groups to sharing the costs of the two oil shocks, as well as those of past excesses. Slowly and hesitantly, certain conditions necessary for the efficient performance of the market system have begun to be restored, mostly through indirect measures, under the protective umbrella of low levels of aggregate economic activities, which dampen expectations.

FRENCH SOCIALISM

With few exceptions this process was still at a very early stage until the first half of the 1980s. Socialist governments of a more orthodox ideological variety were ready to buck the trend even at the time of mounting strains. France was the most outstanding example of this attitude. Ideologically inspired nationalization and other socialist reforms, coupled with the ' last hurrah' of expansive fiscal and monetary policies, were supposed to improve the level of technological sophistication, increase investment, and raise the level of aggregate economic activity. The effects were not those expected, though. It is difficult to assess which were more harmful in the short run (there are no such difficulties with respect to the long run!), but harmful effects were certainly not long in coming.

To their dismay, French socialists learned, like many leftist governments before them, that the rules of the economic game were valid for the left as well. 'Expansion in one country' (to adapt Stalin's slogan), and one with a weak balance of payments position at that, brought about little economic growth but rapid deterioration of the external and internal balance. The government decided to reverse its course, leaving the hunt for the main socialist trophies till some unspecified future. But microeconomic rigidities freshly injected into the French economy through socialist reforms continued to constrain the performance of firms in what had already been the most regulated Western economy. Even the period of economic *rigueur* that lasted till the end of socialist rule, combined with a slightly improved climate for private enterprise and the role of market forces, was not long enough to eliminate all the injurious effects of the early period of unbounded optimism. (A positive by-product of these adverse developments, however, was a marked shift of opinion in favour of economic liberalism in a country with a centuries-long etatist tradition up-held by both right and left.)

There are two more general lessons to be learned from the most recent French flirtation with socialism. The first concerns *the significance of market signals*. Fortunately, no Western economy, including the most extensively regulated ones, has (yet) reached the stage where microeconomic signals are so distorted that they give a *completely* false picture of the business situation. Thus, although the self-correcting, i.e. homeostatic, capacity of the market system has been impaired by the developments described or referred to previously, its signaling ability has not been affected to such an extent. What was lacking at the time was the political will for change. This situation was far more favourable than that of the STEs, where such ability never existed, while the interests of most important segments of the ruling stratum all but excluded a change from planning to the market system. In the STEs costly nonsense can continue for years because non-market signals give a persistently false picture owing to distorted prices and the prevalence of 'imaginative reporting', i.e. distorted quantities (see e.g. Winiecki, 1986a), while market signals are distorted or, in most cases, non-existent. Thus, the costs incurred in the STEs are much higher, correcting periods much longer and living standards are correspondingly affected much more severely.

NEGOTIATED CONSENSUS

The other lesson is about the important role of *consensus*. Even if we leave aside Switzerland, with its unimpaired market system, there are some West European countries whose performance, including with respect to the overwhelming concern of today, employment, is better than that of others. The Federal Republic of Germany and Austria are among the best. But in these countries, whether at the level of industry (West Germany) or country (Austria) there is more often than not a negotiated *consensus* about wage levels and, in consequence, about inflation. As pay restraint is *somewhat* greater in consequence than elsewhere, *consensus* allows firms to stay *somewhat* more profitable and expand. This means, contrary to Pinder's thesis (1982), that even if market rigidities are no different from those in other countries (which is doubtful[33]), a measure of *consensus* with respect to national income shares is important enough to make some difference in performance. Since France is a country where ideological and political cleavages are among the most marked in the Western world, such *consensus* could not have been achieved.

SMALLNESS RESTORED THE EDGE

Portents of change became more marked over time in the economic sphere. It is primarily the electronics complex (computers, electronics applications and communications) that has increasingly been becoming a potent agent of change. Its impact has not been limited to 'standard' changes in productivity, costs and quality, but has begun significantly to affect the market system itself (and, as will be shown, the political system of Western democracy). It is the latter effects, and particularly their potentialities, that are of special interest here.

We begin with some more obvious ones. Greater flexibility is achieved by enterprises. Those with long production runs are able, thanks to reprogrammable machinery, to produce simultaneously more than one product on a production line. On the other hand, enterprises producing in batches, where machinery traditionally operates for no more than 30% of the working time (with the rest spent on retooling, resupplying, etc.) are able to move more smoothly from one product to another.*

But it is not only flexibility, and its second order effects, customization and post-standardization, that are of importance here. Even more significant is reduction in the optimum scale of production. Reprogrammability frees smaller producers from the necessity of changing the machinery on the production line, at very high cost, to turn out a new model or a new product. The best example is the motor industry.

Not long ago experts forecast that in a few years only a couple of giant firms, producing more than 2 million cars each, would be left on the world market. Only these giants, it was said, would be able to bear the huge costs of introducing new models fast enough. Reprogrammable equipment has changed all this. Many firms compete vigorously (in Japan alone there are 9 of them) and — interestingly — it was smaller producers rather than the giants that survived the lean years 1980-1982 in better shape. With the economies of scale handicap removed, or at least weakened, the traditional advantages of smaller firms — flexibility, innovativeness — gave them the edge over their larger competitors. Thus competition intensified on some oligopolistic markets, strengthening the market system itself.

Another trend, namely the expansion of small, high technology-oriented firms, although so far confined largely to the U.S., has begun to make the market system perform better. These firms have not only increased the innovative dynamism of the U.S. economy through their own activities, but also created a more challenging environment for larger firms in their respective industries. Taking heed, Western Europe also started, albeit slowly, to think about the environment in which small, high-technology firms could flourish.

---

*75% of all engineering goods is produced in series no longer than 50 items.

The reappearance of the small innovative firm is not an ephemeral phenomenon. In a world of rapidly changing technology tactics matter as much as if not more than strategy. A moderately good strategy executed quickly counts for more than an excellent one executed slowly. And it is smallness, and the accompanying flexibility, that facilitate this quick execution.

Both developments, reduction of the optimum scale of production and the reappearance of small innovative firms, have had an importance difficult to overestimate. *First,* for more than a hundred years productivity growth went hand in hand with increasing economies of scale. Technological change invariably associated more productive machinery with bigger machinery and lower costs with the three 'S' (standardization, simplification, specialization). Over time factories became larger and enterprises fewer. Thus the electronics complex has changed the established association of technological change and increasingly oligopolistic market structure. *Technological change has turned from an enemy into an ally of the forces of competition.*

Second, the technological dynamism of small firms reestablished the central role of entrepreneurship in spurring innovation and, in consequence, at least questioned (if not actually rejected) the dominant Schumpeterian view of the oligopolistic market structure as most conducive to innovation. Also, it is worth noting that the growing significance of smallness as an advantage has been based upon the technology of tomorrow rather than that of yesterday, as suggested by Schumacher and the like. The message: 'Small is beautiful' is right, but the medium, i.e. obsolete technology, is wrong. Schumacher was evidently right for the wrong reasons.

Beside the trend-changing impact of new technology that strengthens — or, more precisely, has the potential to strengthen — the performance of the market system, some other developments have also strengthened market forces. The latest phase of structural change has been associated with the decline of oligopolistic industries with scale economies that were the mainstay of the long boom of the 1950s and 1960s. The metal producing industries (both ferrous and non-ferrous) are a good example here. For a long time they were growing at a high rate, exceeded only by that of the two leading large groups of industries: chemicals and engineering. But recently they have fallen to the last place but one, growing faster only than the textiles group. Table II/1 shows the changes in some detail. Chemicals stayed at the top, even if with a sharply reduced lead over other groups, but within that group structural change has been occuring as well, with a relative decline in bulk chemicals, based on economies of scale.

These changes would have made themselves felt much more strongly if it had not been for increased governmental intervention in favour of the industries based on economies of scale.

Table II/1

ANNUAL (WEIGHTED) GROWTH RATES OF INDUSTRY GROUPS IN MANUFACTURING IN WESTERN MARKET ECONOMIES (%)

Manufacturing Industry Group	Average annual growth rates		
	1958-1967	1967-1971	1971-1981
Chemicals (incl. refinery products)	9.0	8.3	3.6
Engineering	7.6	5.4	3.1
Food	4.3	4.4	3.1
Stone, clay and glass products	5.3	5.3	2.2
Miscellaneous manufacturing (incl. wood and paper)	5.8	4.4	1.5
Metals (ferrous and non-ferrous)	6.1	4.3	1.2
Textiles (incl. clothing, footwear and leather)	3.8	3.5	0.9
Manufacturing total	6.6	5.2	2.5

Source: CEPII, Economie mondiale: la montee des tensions, Economica, Paris 1983

SHIFT TOWARDS SERVICES

A further portent of change has been a continuous, in many Western countries even accelerated, structural shift towards services. 87% of all new jobs in the U.S. in 1969-1976 were created in the service sector (Birch, 1981). But in the 1970s and early 1980s it was not bureaucracies that grew fastest in this sector. Most of the new jobs created in the U.S. were in private services, mainly in small enterprises, thereby increasing the forces of competition in the American economy.

These underpinnings of economic change, important as they were, would not by themselves have been able to accelerate the slow process of awakening to the extent observable since the early 1980s. A stronger push in this respect came from the now widely recognized *change in political climate* that in some respects preceded economic change. In any case it preceded a recognition of the importance of the latter.

The situation was not that propitious in Western Europe where increased employment in the public sector was the last resort answer to rising unemployment (and an additional burden on the shrinking private sector). But even there, in some countries, such as Germany, private services grew faster than public bureaucracies, thus having a stimulating impact on these economies. Services, especially business services, have their natural base in a healthy, competitive industrial sector and the service economy cannot but be a declining one if there is little to service (see EMF *Report* 1985).

POLITICAL CLIMATE

The era of macroeconomic restraint entered by governments of all political colourings, although forced upon these governments by the economic strains of the day, could not have occurred without changes in the political climate. A feeling of disenchantment with the omnipresence of the government in the economic sphere (and not only there!) had been growing for some time. After all, Jimmy Carter was elected President on roughly the same anti-big government platform that Ronald Reagan continued, with success, promising to 'take the government off people's backs'. This trend began to be visible elsewhere in the West too, most strongly in the United Kingdom. The hope that planning and extensive regulation could solve the complex problems of (interdependent) economies has been evaporating there faster than elsewhere in Europe.

The change of political climate took much longer in France, for Gaullist and semi-Gaullist governments all adhered to a *dirigiste* tradition. But the shock of ideologically motivated nationalization and other intrusions at the micro level, coupled with naive Keynesianism at the macro level, did the job of accelerating disenchantment with leftist ideas. Even the much prized French planning turned out to perform efficiently only in the environment of high and steady growth elsewhere and stable (or slowly rising) prices everywhere. It was an abject failure in the turbulent 1970s and 1980s.

With that change, electoral defeat of the left was certain long before the elections. In Canada, Belgium and Denmark left-leaning parties or coalitions also lost power. Even social democratic or centre-left governments take this change of heart into consideration nowadays. Where they do not, they lose elections. The left's recipes of more intervention, more centralization, more taxes and more egalitarianism, are nowadays beginning to be met with the suspicion that, whether intended or not, they create bigger and ever less flexible bureaucracies decreasingly able to cope with the problems at hand. This is one of the reasons for the electoral defeat of parties with a social democratic orientation, including the Democrats in the U.S. Interestingly, it is the young people who are rejecting the omnipresence of government as a recipe for wellbeing. Reagan's victory over Mondale, for instance, was almost the largest in this age group; the Labour Party's losses between 1979 and 1983 were also largest among young people. Nothing is probably as significant for the waning belief in the government's capacity to solve problems in the economic sphere as the million unemployed who voted for Margaret Thatcher's government in the 1983 election.

This disenchantment has been reinforced and the resultant search (or, more precisely, groping) for solutions facilitated by the strongly articulated view that the arthritis (Blackhurst, 1981), ageing (Kindleberger, 1978), arteriosclerosis (Lindbeck, 1982), or however this particular illness of Western economies is described, has been to a large extent self-inflicted and can be cured only if rigidities are removed. Beside the best known (F. A. von Hayek, Milton Friedman), dozens of other scholars of various theoretical schools but of a similar philosophical orientation, that is to say preference for the market system because of its function as a promotor of efficiency and support for democracy, have become increasingly vocal — and heeded! This exposition of the advantages of the market extended beyond the scholarly world and included, among others, many businessmen who traditionally were rather reluctant to take up the challenge. (There have been exceptions to that reluctance, to be sure. Japanese managers have a tradition of clearly outlining their philosophical *credo* and its economic consequences. Per Gyllenhammer of Volvo, Giovanni Agnelli of Fiat and some others also belong to the same category.)

Similar in effects, although different in methodology, has been the institutional approach to the Western economic system and the accompanying stress upon the harmful role of various 'distributional coalitions' in reinforcing the rigidities of the market system. Privileges of trade union members (as well as various professional groups) have been held up as examples of differentiation of workers' rewards not according to their qualifications, diligence, need of continuous learning or unpleasant job characteristics, but according to the scale of the enterprise and the associated nuisance value of the union. These rewards extended to other areas: working time, additional sickness and unemployment benefits, job security, etc. A sort of dual labour market has begun to take shape, with workers in small enterprises having often higher qualifications, or more unpleasant job characteristics, and nevertheless working longer for less pay. It is trade unions and workers in the already privileged enterprises and industries that press for still shorter working hours, allegedly to increase the number of jobs and absorb a part of the unemployed. However, they usually neglect to include a commensurate nominal wage cut in the proposal so as to make the work sharing compatible with the competitive position of their firms. As FitzRoy (1981) stressed, senior workers, who are not faced with the immediate threat of redundancy, will not accept cuts in working hours *and* wages and, as a result, collective bargaining brings them wage increases as well as shorter working hours, while less senior workers are made more vulnerable to the next round of redundancies, given the weakened cost position of their firms. The large size of their firm makes senior workers impervious to the threat of unemployment, for they have learned that governments usually come to the rescue of large (and only large) enterprises if the threat of failure begins to look imminent. Ironically, this pattern of behaviour by senior workers has often been repeated in declining industries already receiving subsidies.

THE WELFARE STATE

If disenchantment with the omnipresence of government runs deep in a large segment of Western societies, attitudes towards the welfare state have been more ambiguous. Social security coverage, including unemployment benefit, is rightly regarded as a great achievement of the post-war era: a contribution to both the welfare of the labour force and democracy itself. For decades additions to and extensions of social security programmes have been regarded as desirable and progressive.

This attitude has largely survived the resultant excesses and distortions of the welfare system. Always more (incidentally, a title of a French book, *Toujours plus*, by Francois de Closet, 1982) became the motto of left leaning parties, trade unions, and the majority of employees (of varied political colourings). Over time, however, understanding of the fact that the unrestrained expansion of the welfare system has to be accompanied by ever higher taxes, and, consequently, reduced incentives to wealth creation, as well as by an expansion of the 'submerged' economy, has helped to bring about a partial change. Demands for more restrained government spending came to be heard much more often. But there has been a split personality syndrome at work here because demands for less government spending were rarely accompanied by corresponding demands to appropriate less for specific social security programmes. Thus it has been not only left wing politicians and trade unionists, but also large segments of society in general that must share the blame for maintaining unrealistic attitudes (see, for example the empirical work on Denmark by Kristensen (1982)). To repeat the words of Wildavsky (1980), quoted in Kristensen, 'We have seen the enemy and they are us .... '.

The dilemma of a citizen in a welfare state is not an easy one to solve, though. Post-war political programmes of the democratic left tried to insure workers and other employees not only against the effects of cyclical fluctuations in economic activity upon their lot but also against those of 'the hidden face of progress ' — to use the phrase of Alain Leroux (1986) — that is against *insecurity*. But the relentless growth of the welfare system has long ago passed the point of diminishing returns. *The trade-off for maximum security is zero progress.* No incentives, no entrepreneurship, no innovation, no new wealth, as well as shrinking — and therefore increasingly fiercely contested — existing wealth.

But if new wealth is thought to be necessary, as with little exception it is, then changes in the composition and nature of the welfare system cannot be avoided. I say nothing of the level of welfare since the costs of the existing programmes have already forced governments to introduce some cuts (in spite of heated protests by the constituents affected). Sensible and humane solutions to the problem of providing an income floor for all have already been advanced, at the same time reducing some important disincentives to greater work effort.[34] In this respect the welfare system needs to return to its original goals, which assumed income redistribution to the needy, and refrain from redistribution from those slightly above the median to those slightly below it, as well as within these groups but over time, across family sizes, etc.

It is this creeping egalitarianism, financially unsupportable at the levels existing in most extensive welfare systems, that puts an end to wealth creation and ensures a shift of a not inconsiderable amount of human energy towards wealth diversion and a sub-merged economy. No incentive-creating tax cuts are possible in countries where these policies continue. Consequently, such countries will be left behind in terms of international competitive-ness, with all the subsequent effects upon their future level of well-being, as well as the level of welfare provided. Thus, if the well-being of the society as a whole, and support for the needy, are to remain a priority, the continuation of the present composition and nature of the welfare system is self-defeating. But an *a contrario* line of reasoning also applies here: if ideologically inspired egalitar-ianism is at the root of this extensive *redistribution within the middle class-oriented welfare system*, then the price attached to it, namely inevitable decline in the absolute levels of society's well-being and welfare for the needy, should be more conspicuously displayed (as 'advertising standards' rules require).

Certain moves in this direction have already been made by some Western governments. In themselves, however, these moves would count for little if people's attitudes had not been affected by other developments — including those described earlier — that also worked in the same direction, making the price tag more visible to everyone. The resultant intellectual stirrings have become increasingly discernible, especially among the young. Those who vote for liberal and market-oriented policies indicate that a renewed spirit of greater personal responsibility for one's own affairs is slowly catching up with the generation reared by and large in the belief that the welfare state takes care of these affairs from cradle to grave (allegedly at no cost to its personal wellbeing). It is even more encouraging that many young people feel uncomfortable with the welfare system not only because it has turned out to be exceedingly costly but also because they have found that the benefits themselves, along with the desired security, lead to a dependency which stifles initiative.

II.4. ON LASTING UNDERPINNINGS OF CHANGE: SHIFTING ECONOMIC STRUCTURES AND POLITICAL BALANCE

There is, however, an undercurrent of pessimism with respect to the probability of lasting attitudinal change. True, many left-leaning parties lost elections if they happened to be in power when cracks appeared in the solid facade of the increasingly regulated market and redistributive state, but liberal centre-right parties that were in power did as badly, runs the argument. Such reasoning assumes that if they regained power those who lost would return to their old ways regardless of the changed environment and available resources. This pessimism is *not* borne out by recent experience. Many socialist governments, as we have seen, were forced to apply austerity measures, although they were admittedly less ready to tackle the more daunting, and for them politically distasteful, task of overhauling the respective regulatory and redistributive machinery. Also, liberal and market-oriented (so-called centre-right) governments were returned to power in the United Kingdom and the United States with much greater majorities than before, even though they had presided over the deepest recession since the second world war.

CHANGED POLITICAL PREFERENCES

There is enough evidence, then, to maintain that the disenchantment has been, at least in part, with *the way of governance* rather than simply with the governments in power. It would be over optimistic, however, to conclude from this that the effects of the learning process are both universal and permanent. People tend to stick to their views long after these have been proved wrong, too costly or impossible to realize. If this tendency is coupled with the benefits derived personally from the existing way of governance, a lasting attitude change becomes very difficult to achieve. The approaches to change would differ. Some interest groups would fight to maintain the *status quo* they regard as beneficial right now, no matter what costs are imposed upon society (including themselves) in the longer run. Many more would agree in principle with a change in general, but would protest against particular changes (i.e. those affecting them most), as Kristensen's research (1982) tells us. Although the latter approach is certainly transitory, the transition process would be a long one.

Even more important in the longer run, however, are other less easily discernible developments. They concern probable shifts in the balance between those supporting the social democratic practice of more and more extensive regulation of markets, as well as redistributive policies inspired by egalitarianism, and those who believe that the market system is most efficient when regulatory activities enhance its efficiency, rather than run counter to or ignore it, and that the balance between the weakened incentives to create wealth and the increased tendencies to redistribute it ought to be restored. Shifts in favour of such incentives would enhance the market system and reinforce the liberal values of Western democracy in the years to come.

SHIFTS IN EMPLOYMENT

The main source of these shifts in favour of incentives are the significant changes in the structure of employment which are taking place in Western economies. These changes are fourfold:

(1)   shifts in occupational structure;
(2)   shifts in employment structure from large to small enterprises;
(3)   shifts in employment structure towards and within the service sector;
(4)   shifts between employment and self-employment.

To begin with, there has been a long-term shift from blue collar to white-collar jobs demanding higher educational levels. A look at the US gives us a clue in this respect. Table II/2 shows that the proportion of professional, technical and similar workers increased considerably over the 30-year period. So did the proportion of managers and administrators. Together these two groups now make up more than 25% of the total (up from over 15% in 1950). Employees belonging to these groups subscribe more easily to the view that there is a need to restrain government intervention in the businesses in which they play important roles (we leave aside for the moment the professionals and administrators in public services). More often than not, they also feel the effects of high marginal tax rates. This increasingly important segment of society by and large supports liberal-oriented rather than socialist-oriented institutional frameworks and policies.

Table II/2

CHANGES IN OCCUPATIONAL EMPLOYMENT STRUCTURE IN THE UNITED STATES BETWEEN 1950 AND 1982 (%)

Occupation	Percentage of the civilian workforce		
	1950	1970	1982[a]
White collar	36.9	48.2	54.2
Professional, technical and similar	8.5	14.9	17.2
Managers, administrators, except farm	8.9	8.3	11.7
Clerical and similar	12.4	17.9	18.6
Sales workers	7.1	7.1	6.7
Blue collar	40.00	35.9	29.2
Craftsmen, foremen and similar	13.9	13.8	12.3
Operatives and similar	20.1	17.5	12.2
Labourers, except farm and mine	6.0	4.6	4.7
Service workers	10.3	12.8	13.8
Farm workers	12.2	3.1	2.7
Total	99.7[b]	100.0	100.0

[a] October 1982

[b] 0.3 percent was in the category: occupation not reported

Sources: Calculated from: P. M. Blau, 'Implications of Growth in Services for Social Structure', *Social Science Quarterly*, Vol.61, No.1 (June 1980) and *Monthly Labor Review*, September 1982, No.12

On the other hand, the traditional *clientele* of left-leaning parties, blue collar workers, has been shrinking in relative terms. There are, for instance, more professionals and managers now in the American economy than semi-skilled and unskilled workers, i.e. operatives and labourers, and more professionals, managers and clerical workers than traditional blue-collar workers, including craftsmen. In all Western countries that publish the relevant statistics the latter group has decreased recently as a proportion of the total (see Table II/3).

Table II/3

CHANGES IN OCCUPATIONAL EMPLOYMENT STRUCTURE IN SELECTED WESTERN MARKET ECONOMIES BETWEEN 1973 AND 1982 (IN PERCENTAGES OF THE TOTAL)

Occupation	U.S.A.		F.R. of Germany		Sweden		Norway		Australia	
	1973	1982	1973	1982	1973	1982	1973	1982	1973	1982
White collar	48.0	53.8	41.1	46.9	43.9	50.0	38.2	45.7	42.4	47.7
Professional, technical and similar	14.0	17.1	11.1	14.6	21.5	27.3	14.5	19.7	11.4	15.4
Managers, administrators, except farm	10.2	11.6	3.0	3.7	2.0	2.2	4.1	5.7	6.0	6.8
Clerical and similar	17.3	18.5	18.5	19.7	11.5	12.4	9.7	10.6	16.3	17.6
Sales workers	6.5	6.6	8.5	8.9	8.9	8.1	9.5	9.7	8.7	7.9
Blue collar[a]	35.4	29.7	39.5	35.4	35.9	30.1	38.4	32.7	40.8	31.9
Service workers	13.2	13.8	10.3	11.6	13.1	14.0	12.1	13.0	9.0	9.5
Farm workers	3.5	2.7	7.4	5.2	7.1	5.6	11.2	7.8	7.9	7.0

[a] Includes following categories: Craftsmen, foremen and similar; operatives and similar; and labourers except farm.

Source: Calculated from Yearbook of Labour Statistics, 1983

The most telling fact is the changing position of operatives, the core of the strength not only of the political left, but also of the industrial unions. Those employed in large, heavily unionized firms were able to achieve much larger gains in terms of relative wage levels than any other occupational group in most, if not all, Western economies. More often than not, these gains were not commensurate with their level of qualifications, nor with many other established criteria of relative wage levels.

But in the longer run gains that depended first and foremost on bargaining position accelerated labour-saving technological progress. The impact of the electronics complex has made the trend towards reducing direct labour input even stronger. The latest Apple factory (producing the company's latest microcomputer), where direct labour costs are equal to 1% of total costs, will probably be the exception rather than the rule even in the future, but the trend is unmistakable. There will be fewer and fewer operatives as the 1980s progress. If the industrial labour force shrinks, as some forecasts have predicted to about 10% of the total by the year 2000 — operatives as a group will become insignificant, not only as a proportion of the labour force, but also in terms of their economic (and political) position.

Table II/2 shows that in the United States the share of operatives fell as fast in the last decade as in the previous two decades together. This fall has probably been steepest in large firms, and a similar picture may well be found in other Western countries as well.

But at this point we have already encroached upon the second area of change in the employment structure, namely the declining proportion employed in large firms compared with smaller ones. Here again, a long-term trend of more rapid employment increases in the service sector, where establishments are generally smaller than in industry, has been reinforced of late by the impact of the electronics complex. Computerization, robotization, etc., in large enterprises have reduced the numbers employed, and especially the number of operatives. On the other hand, while large firms in industries with scale economies have been reducing employment, small firms have created new jobs at a fast rate. Enterprises on average are smaller and seem likely to shrink further.

SHRINKING SUPPORT FOR THE LEFT

These shifts weaken both left-leaning parties and trade unions. The traditional socialist electorate* is shrinking, not only in num-

---

* That is, those more inclined to vote for communist, socialist, or social-democratic parties.

bers, but also in relative influence. The change in importance is best exemplified by the two miners' strikes in the United Kingdom in 1973/74 and 1984/85. Both were intended not only to increase the benefits enjoyed by a particular occupational group already heavily subsidized by society, but also to regain for the left through strike action what it had lost earlier at the ballot box. The combined effects of shrinking union power and general societal change made the outcomes very different in the two cases.

The diminishing importance of left leaning parties and trade unions also stems from the fact that they are rarely able to present innovative ideas with respect to the problems at hand which, to a considerable extent, are the product of their own past actions. Not surprisingly, this gives them a backward-looking image which is particularly harmful in the eyes of the younger generations. The latter increasingly tend to regard left-leaning parties as representatives of special interest and pressure groups — and not the most needy ones at that.

However, even if industry has traditionally been the core of strength of the left-leaning parties, these parties, and especially social democrats, long ago became national rather than narrowly class-based ones, with a large following outside the blue-collar industrial electorate. This leads us the to the third change in the employment structure, i.e. the shiit towards services and intra-sectoral shifts within the service sector. Here the changes are less unequivocal in terms of consequences for political balance than those analysed above. In general terms, the shift towards services means a shift towards white-collar employment requiring higher eductional levels. As such it is more conducive to liberal (although not necessarily market-oriented) political ideas. At the same time, however, rapid increases in public services have created large bureaucracies which have become 'distributional coalitions' resembling industrial unions. Thus, 'big battalions' have appeared in the service sector as well. To the extent that they associate their relative job security in the public sector with continued social-democratic governance, they may become the primary *clientele* of the left. It is worth noting that this potential new *clientele* would be much more dependent on political choices with respect to the economy than was its predecessor.*

Employment in private and public services grew at about the same rate in the 1960s, but in the 1970s there was a split in the employment pattern. In Western Europe the state played the role of employer of last resort, to reduce unemployment levels, whereas in the US the growth of public services slowed down consider-

---

* This shift could create incentives to expand public-sector, politically dependent jobs as an *electoral* rather than an economic or even an ideological strategy (at least in the short-to-medium term!).

ably while that of private services accelerated. This, incidentally, may help to explain the different political developments in the 1970s, with greater support in the US for those political forces espousing the market cause. However, in the face of large budget deficits any strong expansion of public services in the 1980s seems unlikely. If the US continues to be the trend setter, as it usually has been, an expansion of private services should be expected instead. Employees in the latter, whether highly skilled or not, are more market-oriented. Labour relations are less adversarial and the effort/reward link is stronger, in both cases because of the smaller scale of enterprises and/or establishments. Also, government interventions have usually been beneficial to industrial employees, while those in services bear the costs of these measures.

Moreover, attempts at providing public services more efficiently may encompass privatization of certain services and competition between public and private suppliers of some others. In consequence, one may envisage even absolute decreases of public employment in services. These changes are certainly going to be vigorously resisted, probably with greater success than was the fall in blue-collar employment in manufacturing. In a sheltered sector, not exposed to international competition, arguments on the relative merits or demerits of public versus private provision of services can continue for a long time, so, in the short-to-medium run, it will be faster growth of employment in information-related private services that will slowly shift the balance against the left-leaning, 'three Rs' parties (those favouring regulation, redistribution and resisting change).

SELF-EMPLOYMENT

The last important change in the structure of employment goes beyond employment in the narrow sense and pertains to the increase of self-employment, both in absolute and relative terms (compared with employment). Again, the US has been the forerunner of change. Thus, according to the large scale survey by Fein (1980), in the 1972-1979 period the number of self-employed, both overall and outside agriculture, increased for the first time in decades. It is also interesting that the process accelerated towards the end of the period in question. This change became even more marked in the early 1980s, with the Republican administration creating a more conducive climate for entrepreneurship.

Other Western countries have not registered such a surge of entrepreneurial energy, although the pulse has quickened somewhat in recent years. The role of new small firms in generating innovation, increasing flexibility and providing jobs prompted many West European governments, whether liberal- or social democratic-oriented, to create *some* incentives and remove *some* rigidities hampering the establishment and activities of small firms. The more conducive climate led large industrial firms to support the establishment and expansion of small ones. This has been an effect of the belated recognition of the role of small firms as dynamically growing innovators, whether in the role of subcontractors or competitors. There are signs that a revival of small firms has begun in some West European countries and that they are growing more dynamically than in the past. In Italy, where small firms employing up to 20 persons account for about a third of manufacturing employment, the number of firms increased by about one-third in the last couple of years. This revival is also visible in the United Kingdom, mostly in the south of England. The exact numbers are however in dispute (see *Economist*, 1985, March 25). Even in Japan, where working for a large enterprise in a still dualistic economy is both financially more rewarding and confers greater prestige, talented skilled young professionals are beginning to buck the trend sometimes and establish small firms, individually or in partnership with others. Their numbers, although still relatively small, have been growing markedly of late according to various reports (see, e.g., *Newsweek* 1984, December 3).

It will hardly be disputed that this particular social group, displaying more initiative, risk bearing and innovativeness than any other, is definitely most market-oriented in its views. Entrepreneurs have traditionally been the mainstay of the capitalist private enterprise-based market system and there is no reason for this attitude to have changed over time. The increase in their numbers, absolute and/or relative, means increased support for the liberal and market-oriented changes the signs of which have already been visible in the West.

CONSEQUENCES OF EMPLOYMENT SHIFTS

Taken together, the changes in employment structure analysed above seem to provide solid underpinnings for the political shifts observed in many Western countries in recent years. True, disenchantment with particular governments and, more importantly, with the way of governance have influenced these shifts as well. Nonetheless, the systematic shifts in employment away from blue-collar occupations in industry and from large industrial enterprises, from industrial, on average less skilled, to service, on average more skilled, occupations, and, finally, the change towards increasing self employment, have affected political change indirectly by increasing the liberal and market-oriented electorate. Some of the changes in the structure of employment have been going on for a long time, viz. the decrease of blue-collar jobs in industry or the growing employment in services, but they have accelerated recently. Others are of a more recent vintage (and run counter to the earlier trends of both greater concentration of employment and decreasing self-employment). Together they are steadily changing the political landscape of the West.

What ought to be stressed in conclusion is that the inter-action between economics and politics works both ways. Changes in the employment structure, in themselves the outcome of change in demand and technology, affect the political balance in the direction indicated above. The linkages, however, run, not only from economics to politics, but from politics to economics too. An electorate among which a liberal and market-oriented phil-osophy is more strongly upheld will be more willing to tackle the issues arising out of rigidities injected into the system.

II.5. POSSIBLE SCENARIOS

SCENARIO ONE: THE RESURGENT LIBERAL MARKET-ORIENTED ORDER

The previous three sections have outlined an array of factors — political and economic, short and long-term — that have steadily been affecting the political balance in Western societies. Apart from the swelling public sector in most of Western Europe, all the other factors tend to favour an increasingly liberal market-oriented order, thus reversing the post-war collectivist and etatist trend. The interaction of these factors promises renewed economic dynamism.

To move decisively in this direction some further changes are needed. Both the philosophical underpinnings of the emerging order and the policy measures employed to guide it need refine-ment and extension to make this order more widely acceptable. In this sense the new individualism of the late XX century would be truly emerging rather than re-emerging unchanged from the past. As usual, the changes on the philosophical plane are markedly more difficult to achieve.

What is desirable on the philosophical plane is a *consensus* among the majority (the larger the better) with respect to the fundamental principles of the re-emerging order. To tackle the most difficult one first, we begin with the refocusing of the role of the individual in the economic system. Western civilization has described a rather strange circle in the last couple of decades in this respect, as Kindleberger (1978) pointed out. The individual's role changed from being determined by status or class under the *ancien regime* to being determined by merit under the liberal order and then, with the spread of Mancur Olson's redistributive coalitions, swung back to being determined by status, with participation in benefits won by a given redistributive coalition. There is then an obvious need to refocus attention from the collectives to the individual, to the latter's aspirations and motivation. This refocusing would also mean the re-establishment of a stronger linkage between performance and reward. It is obvious that the corollary of that refocusing would be the acceptance of performance-based inequality of income as a driving force of material (and, although it is not the main concern here, also intellectual) well-being.

In order to gain wide acceptance, this concept, which is part and parcel of the liberal philosophy as applied to the economic sphere, would have to be supplemented by two other concepts of the same philosophical ancestry, namely a guaranteed minimum income and equality of opportunity. In this way the performance-based individualism in a liberal market system *à la* Friedman, von Hayek, de Jouvenel and others would be moderated by equity considerations. (For a more detailed account of various shades of economic liberalism, see, among others, Chapman, 1980).

The provision of both an income floor and the so-called collective goods (education, health, etc.) would, however, have to satisfy the cost-effectiveness criterion. This would entail a different view of the role of government. Thus, the next important philosophical change would concern the redefinition of that role. The redefinition would have to extend far beyond income distribution, though.

GOVERNMENT EFFICIENCY

The widespread disenchantment with the ability of government to solve various interrelated economic, social and other problems and the popular demand to take the government off people's backs would have to be transformed into a new recognition not only of what the government should, but also of what it *can* do efficiently, as well as of *how* it could proceed in so doing.

Thus, at the micro level government has been proved to be at a competitive disadvantage in producing anything, goods or services, that could alternatively be produced by private enterprise. Also, selective interventions in the market place by government could be justified only if they create a more encouraging environment for private initiative and entrepreneurship or, at the extreme, if they facilitate structural change. But then their precise nature would become very important. Measures should be allowed only if they were not firm-specific, that is not aimed at selecting winners or propping up losers. This was tried in both Western and Soviet-type economies, and it failed, while Japanese interventions directed at a *class of enterprises* that later selected winners and losers among themselves through competition proved to be more successful.

Another consequence of acknowledging government's comparative disadvantage would be acceptance of the idea of privatization, as far as the production of goods and the provision of some services is concerned. Alternatively, or simultaneously, the injection of a healthy dose of competition between private and public bodies in the provision of services should be encouraged. The specific forms of privatization could vary. The present privatization programing of the British Conservative government is but one solution among many and not necessarily the one most conducive to the extension of the liberal market-oriented order.[35]

We have already pointed out in the introduction to this part of the book that one school of recent politico-economic thinking has demolished the socialist mystique of the benevolent state, selfless public servants and costless intervention. The welfare costs of political interventions turned out to be of a much higher order of magnitude than the costs of market failure. It has also added to our knowledge not only about the limits to what government can do but also about the limits to the means which it can use to achieve these limited goals efficiently.

Thus, ensuring that the costs of externalities are reflected in the market-place ought to proceed as much as possible through cost-effective pricing rather than through regulation and control procedures (on this point, see e.g. Shultz, 1981). The pricing methods proposed and recently tried with respect to pollution, like effluence fees and, even less costly, marketable discharge permits, are a case in point (Oates, 1984).

Even in the area where government clearly has the strongest comparative advantage, i.e. raising and distributing money, the cost-effectiveness requirements would demand redefinition of the means. The direction of change would have to be away from complicated and cumbersome bureaucratic procedures and towards simpler solutions (like, for example, the old Milton Friedman idea of negative income tax). Altogether with respect to government intervention caution should be the watchword and, as one critic put it succinctly, 'the presumption should be against it' (O'Dowd, 1980).

LABOUR MANAGED FIRMS

The set of philosophical guiding principles would have to entail the abandonment of yet another cherished socialist myth

— that of the intrinsic value of the labour-managed firm. It was well defined private property rights, together with political freedom, that decided where innovation explosion and industrial revolution took place in the past (see North and Thomas, 1973). Also, it is the fact that property rights have been least distorted in the United States that has contributed to the beginning of what many regard as the next innovation explosion and industrial revolution precisely in that country (and not elsewhere).

Various forms of worker participation in management, including actual self-management, blur the lines of property rights and introduce inefficiencies not found in privately owned capitalist firms. It is often forgotten that if and when self-management was proposed, as in Yugoslavia, or even more so in Poland in 1980-1981, it was due not so much to the workers' strongly felt need to participate in managing their enterprises but to recognition of the inferiority of a Soviet-type command economy and unwillingness (Yugoslavia) or political impossibility (Poland) of reintroducing the superior, capitalist, private enterprise-based market economy.[36]

No less importantly, it is not at all certain that some important workers' needs would really be satisfied through workers' participation in management. The leap from the existence of workers' alienation in large business organizations to the assumed workers' need for participation in *management* is not justified on theoretical or empirical grounds. As a recent piece of research on America's best-run companies (Peters and Waterman, 1982) shows, what makes employees tick is the need to stand out (be recognized as an outstanding performer) and to be a part of a team (a measure of conformity in return for the sense of belonging to a larger meaningful whole)[37] at the same time. However, outstanding performance also comes from having a measure of control over one's own immediate working environment, and being listened to attentively, as well as being encouraged to be creative in the fulfillment of the shared goals of a business organization. This is also the way to stimulate willingness to bear risk, to innovate and to be enterprising. Participating in management would probably be as distant from these universal needs as self-management is for a Yugoslav worker's needs now.

Besides, recent research in organization theory points out that not all workers even want to satisfy these needs within business organizations (for a review of the literature see Pitt Booth, 1983). Participation *in management* in the West is a politically inspired idea that serves the left as an alternative route to or reinforcement of political power and has little to do with the revealed needs of employees in business organizations. At the same time, in purely economic terms, it is a clearly retrogressive alternative for the West (it may not be so for the East, where a capitalist market economy may not only be impossible politically but, after becoming possible politically, may not be feasible economically for a long time).

'NEW INDIVIDUALISM'

Growing recognition and acceptance of this thinking would transform the disenchantment with government's role in the economy and the renewed interest in the market system into lasting philosophical underpinning of a liberal market-oriented order. This 'new individualism', reinforced by changing patterns of demand and technology-driven economic and political changes, would also be better attuned to the individual's needs in the working environment and beyond (first of all in the local community).[38]

Support for the market system and the liberal order which reinforces it would increase over time as economies pursuing this path more decisively would show comparatively better performance both in macroeconomic (economic growth, employment, inflation, trade balance) and microeconomic terms (flexibility, innovation, entrepreneurship).

What is extremely important in this respect is a renewed — and more conscious — acceptance of the rather simple but partly forgotten truth that life means change. Consequently, in the economic field too, there must be structural change and accompanying factor mobility. In the specific context of the late XX century it also means, to a very large extent, change from transforming materials to transforming information. That makes structural change, and especially the present blue-collar labour adjustment, more traumatic than in the past. However, this is not an argument against change, against life itself, although it may be one for thoughtful, specifically circumscribed government intervention facilitating that adjustment.

Incidentally, we have been stressing the economic efficiency advantages of a liberal market-oriented order in comparison with a social democratic one. These advantages are substantial but a 'new individualism', as we have dubbed the philosophical underpinnings of the order, promises something else as well. It promises also greater fulfillment of human needs both in the working environment and beyond.

A more innovative workforce, more willing to bear risk, is not only more efficient but also more satisfied with what it is doing. Those who want to stand out, to be outstanding performers, have a much greater chance to fulfill their ambitions than under initiative-stifling, egalitarian-oriented etatism. Also, recognition of the variety of areas where these needs may be fulfilled beyond business organization will reinforce the diversity which is an important ingredient of life itself. In comparison with the *institutional boredom* (to borrow a phrase from Zbigniew Brzezinski) of the uniformity imposed from above in the collectivist-etatist system, the new individualism promises also to be more intellectually rewarding. Thus, it is not only consumption, i.e. living standards in the narrower sense, but also satisfaction from one's own work effort, i.e. a part of living standards in the broader sense, that will make greater progress.

SCENARIO TWO: HALTING AND HESITANT MOVEMENT IN THE SAME DIRECTION

The outline presented in the preceding subsection should be regarded as an optimistic 'straight path'. Such scenarios materialize rather rarely. The underpinnings of a new — or even a renewed — order do not become acceptable either quickly or uniformly. They are usually absorbed bit by bit, issue by issue, social group by social group. As things stand now, there are still numerous and politically active believers in various shades of egalitarianism and the whole collectivist-etatist value hierarchy. Even more numerous in Western countries are people who benefit (or think they benefit) from redistributive policies applying those values in practice.

REDISTRIBUTIVE COALITIONS

The resistance to achieved income and status, especially from well organized 'redistributive coalitions', may be very strong and disruptive. The term 'disruptive' has been chosen carefully. When the liberally inclined political scientist Rolf Dahrendorf applies the term 'defenders of declining groups' to Western trade unions, or the socialist-inclined French sociologist Alain Touraine admits that the parties of the left came to power with an ideology and social base that belong to the past, they are saying the same two things. First, that the power base of both left-leaning parties and trade unions is shrinking, and second, that neither left-leaning parties nor trade unions are able to offer much in the way of new ideas. They may resist change, sometimes in a very disruptive and costly manner, they may slow it down or even reverse it for the time being, but the probability that they will be able to stop it forever and continue along the well trodden and increasingly burdensome path of collectivist and etatist policies is rather low, while their ability to generate new ideas is even lower.

It is nevertheless important to survey the most contested ideas and policies for a more market-oriented order. Such a survey may reveal the strength and durability of resistance, as well as the areas of possible accomodation on the basis of experience drawn from both the continuing resurgence of the market system and the mounting costs of resistance to change.

To begin with, it is policies increasing income differentials that come under strongest attack. On the political plane the old socialist/populist cry that the rich get richer while the poor get poorer has been heard more often of late in those countries where modest reductions in extremely high marginal tax rates and various other disincentives have been attempted. The left's fixation with income distribution (differentials, shares, etc.), at the expense of growth,[39] prevents it from recognizing that the picture is very different in absolute rather than relative terms. Better rewarded risk-bearing activities increase wealth by much more than the sum of the rewards for those who bear the risk, leaving the rest of society absolutely better off. The philosophical conversion of avowed egalitarians may be very slow, although not impossible. However, this conversion may proceed at a rather less slow pace as those who benefitted in the past from income redistribution discover that there is less and less wealth to redistribute, while liberal, growth-oriented policies elsewhere are bringing increases in real incomes and creating new jobs. On a more practical plane, these policies may be disrupted by trade unions' claims for a greater share of income and/or demands to restore old differentials.

Here the problem is fraught with more dangerous consequences, for 'redistributive coalitions' possess quite considerable nuisance capacity *vis-à-vis* societies. That capacity can be — and has been — used to show that accomodation of union demands is, after all, less costly than resistance (in the short term, of course). The probability of such disruptive action is somewhat lower nowadays, though, after a few years of restrictive macroeconomic policies almost everywhere in the Western world. And their chances of success, in the sense of policy reversal, seem to be even lower, given the possibility of renewed macroeconomic restraint measures and wider recognition of the harmful effects of accomodation to union demands. In other words, greater public support may embolden weak, liberal-leaning governments with slim majorities to pursue policies supporting the new individualism.

WAGE DIFFERENTIALS

No less disruptive, however, may be attempts at restoring old wage differentials among groups of workers in the face of changing productivity growth rates in different industries, as in the inflation model presented by, among others, the present author (1978, 1980, 1986c). Here, only a growing *consensus* on the necessity of change in wage differentials in line with greater productivity increases and related greater efforts at mastering fast changing technologies may improve the situation over time. Such a *consen-*

sus is more possible now than in the past because of the shift of productivity growth (and wage growth) leadership from heavily unionized industries based on economies of scale to little union-ized ones, driven by technological innovation and exhibiting a more cooperative industrial relations style. Thus, over time, a change for the better may be expected with respect to this type of disruptive behaviour. There is a possibility, though, that the pro-cess may be facilitated by the greater self-restraint displayed by unions in industries based on economies of scale as these industries shrink rapidly.

Altogether this pushing and pulling — not so much at but rather around the market place — is going to continue, although it will become less intense. Its persistence will vary inversely with the already growing understanding that in a market economy the most important market, i.e. the labour market, cannot be petrified and shielded from change regardless of what is happening in the rest of the system.

INDUSTRIAL ROMANTICISM

What will also fade over time is the present curious romantic view of industrial employment[40] that for some rather obvious reasons is limited to manual jobs in smokestack industries. No-body seemed to be unduly alarmed when jobs in clothing or textiles began to disappear more than a decade ago in industrial-ized Western economies. The spectre of deindustrialization (which has been shown to be false with respect to the US, for example by Lawrence, 1983) was raised only when certain industries based on economies of scale began to loose their competitive position on the world market. The demands for protection were raised in unison by strong 'redistributive coalitions' encompassing both trade unions and management in the threatened industries.

SHORTER WORKWEEK

The issue of unemployment, however, will not go away until the early 1990s. In view of this, various schemes to mitigate it deserve thorough evaluation. The least effective will be a shorter workweek without commensurate nominal wage cuts. The in-evitable outcome of that will be less employment due to compet-itive pressures resulting from higher labour costs or, where labour cost increases are absorbed internally, from reduced ability to generate funds for investment. A shorter workweek benefits only those already in work who have seniority levels which shield them from the redundancy to which their actions inevitably lead: For this reason the demand for a shorter workweek without a com-mensurate wage reduction will be put forward, and sometimes it will succeed (as with the German metalworkers in 1984).

Less contentious would be a rise in the school-leaving age with the additional post-secondary education aimed at the development of functional skills necessary for tomorrow's jobs. These are first of all skills related to information processing. In the communications and electronic data processing subsector the growth of new jobs is projected to increase the fastest (see Table II/4). Also, the same skills will be necessary in other subsectors of services where there will be an above average increase in new jobs, like financial services, health care services, etc. In actual fact these skills will become an important ingredient in most jobs, whether in the above subsectors or elsewhere.

FLEXIBLE WORKFORCE

More contentious would be the idea of a flexible workforce, with a shrinking core of ever more versatile full-time employees, and an expanding proportion of part-time employees, whose number of working hours would be adjustable to demand, and 'external' employees, hired on short term contracts, individually or collectively. In static terms the same workload would be spread among more people, thereby reducing unemployment, but in dynamic terms greater flexibility would also help to bring about higher economic growth and higher demand for labour. There are obvious advantages in such a solution that need not be enumerated here, but there are also disadvantages, especially with regard to old age (and invalidity) pensions, that may necessitate changes in social security rules (and probably also funding) to accomodate greater fluctuations in earnings.

The resistance may come for other reasons, though. Trade unions may resist the idea (which outside the smokestack industries is already becoming a reality) of differentiating the degree of job security *within* firms. It should be remembered, however, that *de facto* differentiation of job security between firms and industries has always existed, typically with a lower degree of security for workers (and owners!) of smaller firms selling in more competitive markets. It is in large firms in concentrated industries that virtual job guarantees were established over the last quarter of a century. In reality the job guarantees were to the advantage only of the more senior workers because higher wages in the face of stagnant or falling demand resulted inevitably in redundancies, which hit the less senior workers hardest. Thus, even in firms and industries with high job security *de facto* differentiation is a fact of life.

HIGH TAXES ON RAW MATERIALS

More far-reaching is the idea advanced by a McKinsey consultant, Max Geldens, *(Economist*, 28 June 1984): He coupled the usual supply-side proposal of much lower and less steeply progressive income taxes with high excise taxes on energy and industrial raw materials, especially non-renewable ones. This would refocus technology away from reducing labour content to reducing the material and energy content of goods and services. Its implementation would inevitably alter the structure of demand. The direction of change would please conservationists but not, for obvious reasons, those in resource-intensive industries, whether managers or workers. The resistance would be strong, for they are the industries where demand is by and large already stagnant or falling.

It is workers in these heavily unionized, resource-intensive industries and industries based on economies of scale that constitute the most intractable part of the unemployment problem. They are certainly a declining group. All forecasts indicate a steep fall in employment in these industries (for manufacturing as a whole, see Table II/4). Their political clout, however, is disproportionately great and with it their ability to slow down necessary change at the expense of society at large. The resistance to change will be all the stronger as wages in these industries are generally way above average while skills are at or below average. Given the discrepancy between wage levels and skill levels, the probability of finding equally well paid industrial jobs is in fact nonexistent. (For this group even retraining schemes may not help very much, for equally well paid jobs in the service sector require different educational levels.) Any solutions will necessarily be of a partial nature (early retirement, subsidized upgrading of educational level for younger workers enabling them to acquire new skills, shift to part-time jobs with incomes augmented by partial unemployment benefit schemes, etc.).[41] There is no denying, however, that after enjoying an above-average share of the fruits of economic growth for some 20-30 years this group faces a period with a below-average share. New well-paid jobs will be created elsewhere in the economy and for the most part beyond the reach of redundant operatives and unskilled workers from these industries.

RESISTANCE TO CHANGE

The inevitable adjustment may be complicated by the fact that workers in these industries constitute the core of the original *clientele* of the social-democratic parties in the West. Thus, various measures may be expected from left-leaning governments petrifying existing structures. Also, some obvious non-solutions to the un-

Table II/4

FORECAST CHANGES IN SECTORAL AND SUBSECTORAL
EMPLOYMENT STRUCTURE IN THE UNITED STATES
BETWEEN THE YEARS 1980 and 2000 (in %)

Sectors and subsectors	Percentage of the civilian workforce	
	1980	*2000 (forecast)*
Goods producing sector		
Agriculture	2.0	1.5
Fishing	0.4	0.4
Forestry	0.8	0.8
Mining	1.0	1.0
Manufacturing	21.0	11.5
Construction	4.8	4.8
Subtotal	30.0	20.0
Service sector		
Financial services	7.6	8.0
Communications/electronic services	1.4	6.5
Transportation	3.1	3.0
Health care	7.1	8.0
Education	7.6	7.0
Restaurant/food services	7.1	8.0
Wholesale/retail trade	13.8	14.0
Hotel/motel services	1.1	2.0
Leisure services	1.1	3.0
Misc. private services	2.4	2.5
Utility/government services	17.7	18.0
Subtotal	70.0	80.0
Total	100.0	100.0

Source: D. A. Collier, 'The Service Sector Revolution: The Automation of Services', *Long Range Planning*, Vol. 16, 1983, No.6.

employment problem may be applied, like a shorter workweek (the failure of this was well demonstrated in France), public sector job creation schemes, etc. All this, where social democrats are in power or where unions are able to exert strong pressure on weak governments, may slow down or temporarily halt structural change and with it the shift towards the more competitive, flexible and market-oriented economic order.

The stress is on the word 'temporarily', though. Demand for the products of these industries is in any case either rising only slowly or stagnant or falling. At the same time productivity is increasing fast (attempts to stop this would result in an even greater fall in demand due to lost competitiveness). That in itself affects structural change, in spite of all subsidies, tax reliefs and import protection measures.

Under the above circumstances governmental measures increasing competitiveness may not be initiated, or may be successfully resisted. Some of these, like deregulation, may be put off for fear of their initial adverse impact on jobs; some others, like privatization or increased competition between private and public institutions in providing certain services may be unacceptable to left-leaning governments for ideological reasons. However, here again technological change and the shift in demand will exert pressure in the desired direction. In the goods producing sector new, innovative, small firms will be increasing competitive pressure on large oligopolists, making the latter more cost conscious and forcing them at least to reduce overmanning. Competition will also increase due to the continuous blurring of the demarcation lines between product markets as a result of technological change. Various oligopolists from previously segmented product markets will be forced to compete not only against innovative new entrants but also against each other in more broadly defined multi-product markets.

The absence of efficiency-increasing measures, like privatization or competition between private and public institutions in services, will not halt the change in employment structure. The demand for information-related services will continue to increase at a high rate, increasing employment in non-traditional services. This growth in demand from private firms and the general public will be met mostly by small, private firms and self-employed professionals working from home rather than by large, often state owned, enterprises. Moreover, tight public sector budgets may force public bodies to depend increasingly on sub-contracted private services rather than on their own (much more costly) permanent departments. Thus, although more slowly than under the 'straight path' alternative, efficiency will nevertheless be on the increase.

An important factor reinforcing the often slow and halting march toward the strengthened market system and resultant greater efficiency will, as usual, be the demonstration effect. Higher growth, employment and real incomes in countries with a more liberal market-oriented order could bring about either a change of government or a change of heart which may be only temporary on the part of existing left-leaning governments. In either case progress would be accelerated (in the latter case temporarily only).

We have a somewhat ironic paradox here. The further any Western economy were to travel down this road of strengthening the market system at the micro level, the more efficient macroeconomic policies would be. At the same time, however, they would be less urgently needed, because better functioning markets and a policy environment supportive of innovation, entrepreneurship and risk bearing in general would more easily reduce the layer of Keynesian-type unemployment without strong macroeconomic stimulation. On the other hand, strong stimulation would be most needed in countries where a lack of *consensus* on the fundamental requirements of an efficiently functioning market system perpetuated stagnation, inflation and unemployment. But in the latter countries such stimulation either would not be applied for fear of renewed wage pressures or if applied, would generate these self-same pressures, dissipating the stimulus through higher wages and cost inflation. This would be yet another proof of the old adage that those who have learned nothing from the past are bound to repeat their mistakes.

SCENARIO THREE: FROM DECREASINGLY COMFORTABLE STATUS QUO TO DECLINE (WITH SOME HAYEKIAN OVERTONES)

The scenario outlined below is improbable for the West as a whole. It is not even probable for Western Europe. However, it cannot be excluded on *a priori* grounds and this is why it has been described explicitly here. We begin with George Shultz's caustic dictum: 'When things get bad enough, people will do even obvious and sensible things.' Let us assume that the 1980-1982 recession and its aftermath made the economy a little more balanced. A period of macroeconomic restraint at home and abroad moderated (temporarily) unions' wage claims. Somewhat improved profits slowly began to be translated into investments (slowly, given low capacity utilization levels and uncertainty owing to past experience with governmental intrusions). Higher levels of economic activity abroad boosted exports. Energy saving technologies kept oil prices from increasing in spite of renewed, albeit slow, economic growth.

Budget deficits began to diminish. Under these circumstances gradual downward correction of real wages to make up for past excesses and changed relative energy prices ceased to be *à la mode.*

Left-leaning governments, or weak governments under strong pressure from the unions, might decide that things were no longer bad enough to justify doing obvious and sensible things. Especially as these sensible things are not only difficult but (for them) politically distasteful. Thus, instead of removing or at the very least substantially reducing the macroeconomic rigidities which weaken the performance of their national economies, they would opt for palliatives in the next phase. The consequences would be felt very quickly throughout the economy.

'BUSINESS AS USUAL'

Given the prevailing political climate, the 'redistributive coalitions' would decide it was 'business as usual' and press (successfully) for another wage increase unrelated to productivity — and/or profit. But in open economies it would again be those already employed — and the more senior at that — who gained in the longer term. The less senior would not survive the following recession and would be made redundant. Unemployment would rise as a result, firms would become less cost-competitive relative to those in countries where earlier scenarios prevailed, and, consequently, taxes would be raised again to compensate everybody (to an extent).

But incentives to work would suffer once more. Productivity would decline or not increase much in spite of large investments made possible by overgenerous incentives to invest. Hidden intra-firm unemployment would increase. Costs and prices would rise, cutting demand for domestically produced products. Both employment and the external balance would be adversely affected. Under the circumstances an obvious non-solution to the unemployment problem could be adopted, namely a shorter workweek (without a commensurate wage cut, of course). Such a move would again increase real wages and require more subsidies and more taxes.

But an important *caveat* should be added. It is *large* firms, employing a large number of (usually unionized) workers, that would receive compensation due to the political clout of both management and unions. And it is there that labour, or a large part of it, is shielded for a long time from the unemployment consequences of such developments. Smaller firms, which cannot count on such generosity, shed labour immediately or go out of business. This pattern has been repeated again and again.

The effects would thus be adverse not only with respect to the level but also the structure of employment. Excessive wages in large firms would result, slowly but surely, in job losses by attrition. No new workers would be engaged during recovery periods and whatever extra demand appeared would be satisfied by higher productivity and overtime work. Few new firms would be established, given the strong disincentives to entrepreneurship, and a greater number of firms would disappear. The innovative and employment creating advantages of small business would thus be forgone. With falling employment, the clamour for more subsidies to large firms to slow down the fall in the number of jobs and for higher public employment (including various public works schemes) would increase.

The distorted employment pattern would have the strongest negative effects on the young. Not only would jobs for new entrants to the labour market become scarcer but they would also increasingly have to acquire their experience and job skills in decreasingly efficient, uncompetitive firms permanently dependent upon government subsidies. An alternative would be sheltered employment in the public sector. In both cases their ability to adjust to changes in skill requirements would be impaired.

At this point we should consider the consequences of the changing *clientele* of the left-leaning parties for this scenario. Whether as an employer of last resort in the face of the declining competitiveness of the private sector *vis-à-vis* that in more market-oriented Western and developing economies, or because of an ideological preference for publicly provided services, the public sector would expand, probably dramatically. Sheltered from international competition, its size is almost entirely dependent upon political choices. Thus, it would be ready to block administratively the competitive entry of private entrepreneurs prepared to supply the services it provided at lower cost.

PUBLIC SECTOR EMPLOYEES

Public sector employees and their unions would become 'redistributive coalitions' with a vested interest in maintaining and expanding the public sector with its leisurely and undemanding work pace. Quite naturally they would be more willing to vote for those parties that promised to maintain the sheltered nature and expand or at least maintain the size of the public sector.[42] Given their numerical preponderance over the traditional *clientele* of the left, their impact upon the political choice between reinforcement of the market system and continuing on the collectivist/etatist course could become greater.

Their impact could also become more pernicious, since some

public administrators would try to slow down or halt altogether efficiency-increasing changes that would threaten their own number and power to regulate. The democratic political process makes the bureaucracy's grip less destructive than under totalitarianism but it would nonetheless adversely affect measures designed to strengthen the market system.

However, it would stretch the argument too far to assume that the propensity of either old or new *clientele* to vote for the left-leaning parties is unlimited. The trade-off between their job security and living standards would become increasingly visible in the senario under consideration. If income taxes were taking away 60-85% of gross income (a *present* Swedish reality; see Lundberg, 1983) their purchasing power with respect to market-distributed goods would be eroded while their returns in the form of publicly provided goods and services would also decline given the adverse cost/benefit relationship in their provision. At that point, the larger, non-ideologically motivated part of the *clientele* of the left would probably be ready to change its political allegiance.

Under such circumstances other obstacles could arise, though. Even if the consequences of the fundamental trade-off became starkly visible to all, there might still be no move away from the inefficient system. The reason is that under 'advanced' collectivism various kinds of intertemporal, inter- and intra-generational, inter- and intra-group redistribution would make the reversal extremely difficult, since many of the beneficiaries (victims) would be unable to calculate the benefits (losses) of such a move. They would add to the numbers of those who consciously opposed any change towards the resurgent market system.

INTERNAL DYNAMICS

Let us return to the internal dynamics of this scenario. Increasing costs, underinvestment, or more probably, misdirected investment and weak innovative performance, would be less and less able to maintain a satisfactory export performance. Export markets would be lost while import penetration would increase, albeit slowly, due to rising and successful pressures for protection. Further job losses would not be prevented. The effects of compensation and protection would increasingly distort factory and goods markets. Despecialization would become more frequent, worsening the net to gross output ratio. The smaller the national economy affected by this scenario, the greater the scope for falling efficiency and real incomes. Even without exogenous disturbances, economic growth, slow even at the beginning of the scenario, would cease altogether. With higher costs resulting from misdirected investments, and resources locked in obsolete industries and ailing firms, increasingly equal real incomes would have to fall (and so would the real value of unemployment benefits, pensions, etc.).

It is probably at this point that the political *clientele* would desert the left-leaning parties in power *en masse*. Equality in decline is not what most of them, except perhaps true socialist believers, prefer. Quite probably the switch in voters' allegiance would be more decisive than the one that occurred in the early 1980s. It would also be facilitated by two further developments, to which we now turn.

First, the free flow of information would have a positive demonstration effect showing that improved market performance, greater personal initiative and risk bearing, although bringing about structural change through Schumpeterian creative destruction, also raise living standards[43] and give those who work, self-employed and employed alike, much greater job satisfaction. The same free flow of information would create a negative demonstration effect for it would be palpably obvious that socialists lack any serious alternatives to liberal, market-oriented solutions.

A case in point is the report by trade union economists called *Keynes Plus Participatory Democracy* (1979) that recommended macroeconomic expansion, price controls, state-determined investment levels in industries and firms, as well as worker participation in investment decisions and 'a fairer share of the income' resulting from investments. The *déjà vu* qualities of the macroeconomic proposals are obvious to everybody. The participation proposals may be less obvious but are no more helpful. Economic theory and Yugoslav practice both prove that labour-managed firms display a capital intensive bias.[44] Thus, where unemployment is the main problem, such a solution would be counterproductive (even if we leave aside the other problems it would create). The Swedish centralized alternative, a union-managed investment fund, smacks too much of central planning: in few areas has it failed as miserably as in investment.

Where socialist proposals abandon their standard solutions tried and found wanting in the West or in the East, they range from funny to frightening. A case in point may be those formulated by Lars Ingelstam (1983). He properly recognized that the Swedish type of welfare state needs a high growth capitalist open economy and will not have one in the future (although for him the causes are exogenous, rather than endogenous, that is to say the impact of collectivist and etatists policies upon the private sector, making it less able to compete internationally). Thus he stressed the need to search for an alternative, but when he moved from general principles to practical recommendations the results were a flop. He proposed, for example, local control of some recreational services and eventually takeover production of recreational goods, much as the British cooperative movement tried and failed in the XIX century (for the causes of the failure, see, for example, Wiles, 1977). With respect to food supply he stressed the benefits of .... own food production by households *à la* Soviet type economies, evidently forgetting that small private plots there are a protection against starvation in the face of the dismal performance of state and collective farms. They are *not* cost-effective *vis-à-vis* private farming. And in spite of all the STEs' experience Ingelstam even proposed collectives above household level! That collectivist streak was also visible in proposals concerning housing, car pools, etc., some recommended as voluntary and others to be mandated by local government *fiat*. On the not purely economic plane proposals for media controls by 'popular movements' smack more of a Soviet- rather than a Western-type approach, as typified by the 'interest of the people' argument in favour of censorship.

But these new leftist irrelevancies and temptations would (we may hope) be disregarded by the majority of the social-democratic *clientele*. At the same time, mainstream proposals would amount to the conceptual defence of the decreasingly comfortable *status quo*. This negative demonstration effect would contribute to the erosion of the political base of the left.

The second of the developments affecting voters' allegiance would be a by-product of collectivist-etatist policies themselves. Slack performance in the public provision of services is making them increasingly costly. In some Western countries various privatization schemes and private competition with public bodies would be worked out as the least economically costly solutions. In other countries these would be blocked by the strength of the public sector's 'redistributive coalitions'.

But even in the latter countries, where political factors would prevent such solutions, erosion of the public sector would be taking place anyway. The increasing cost of publicly provided services is already giving rise to an informal sector in public services as well. Its expansion increases the cost of the services still publicly provided even further. That would affect the problem in question in two ways. Former recipients of publicly provided services, now recipients of those of the informal sector, would be less willing to vote for the collectivist-etatist option. Also, such a change would further lower revenues, leading to increasing taxes and hence to decreasing work incentives, stagnation and decline. In the longer term perspective the latter would also affect voters' perception of the desirability of collectivist-etatist solutions.

Realistically, we could end this scenario here. The shift away from the left-leaning parties would be large enough to sweep them from power for quite a long time. But assume for a moment that in one or two countries egalitarianism as a goal prevailed over prosperity (and individual satisfaction). What would these countries look like in a dozen years or so? We would probably see a mixture of the features we see now in import substitution-oriented LDCs and STEs. Both sub-optimal production runs and over-employment would be found in the private sector. So would centralization, with all the accompanying additional waste of production factors. Isolation from the world market would proceed apace, given the increasingly uncompetitive nature of such an economy, devoid of incentives to innovate or even to work. The main difference relative to those two groups of countries would be the direction of change, as both import substitution-oriented LDCs and STEs have been at least attempting to modify their institutional features in a search for greater market and export orientation (that the latter did not succeed owing to the interaction between political and economic systems is another matter). An additional difference would be higher absolute levels from which decline began, although the direction of change would be the same in this case.

The internal dynamics of the scenario in question would lead towards ever greater centralization and lower efficiency. The rising costs of despecialization and misallocation of resources would generate — within the etatist frame of thinking — calls for further regulation. There would be increasing, albeit unsuccessful, attempts to stop the spread of the informal sector. But, under the circumstances of higher and higher costs in the decreasingly open economy, a *larger*, not a smaller, 'submerged' economy would be the reaction to multiplying disequilibria. A vicious circle would arise, as the decreasing efficiency of the increasingly regulated market would generate demands for more regulation (on this point, see Kornai, 1984, with respect to general issues and Carlsson, 1980, with respect to the Swedish case on the threshold of the 1980s).

A socialist-governed but still democratic country would reach a dangerous crossroads. The free inflow of information would be showing that things were different — and manifestly better — in countries that had chosen the liberal and market-oriented alternative. Also, the unimpeded outflow of competence, as Asar Lindbeck (1984) puts it, would be continuing. The emigration of researchers, engineers, entrepreneurs and others valuing individualism and disliking the stifling uniformity would over time weaken the country's already falling competitive prowess. The totalitarian temptation for left-leaning governments to stop both the inflow of ideas and the outflow of people would become very strong at that point. If not rejected, it would reinforce the economic decline and conceivably open a Hayekian road to serfdom as well. Many would later discuss whether those countries were destined to cease to be a part of the prosperous and democratic West. However this scenario would illustrate how the German philosopher Arthur Schopenhauer was right in saying that what people call 'destiny' is usually the consequence of their own acts of folly.

II.6. IN PLACE OF CONCLUSIONS

In considering alternative economic futures and their under-pinnings, I have put strong emphasis on ideologically motivated policy choices. This emphasis was not accidental. It is this moti-vation that may be the main factor determining not only the speed (as in the first and second scenarios) but also the direction (as in the third scenario) of economic change. For the scenario of de-cline clearly shows that the technologically reinforced changes in production and employment structures leading to shifts in politi-cal alignments and — on the feedback principle — to the resurg-ence of the market system and a more liberal political order are probable but not inevitable developments.

CAPITALISM vs. SOCIALISM

Contemporary history has decided what has been theoretically debated for decades, i.e. the competition in terms of efficiency between capitalism and socialism. Capitalism has clearly won and if socialism is advertised nowadays in the West it is no longer for its efficiency but for its claimed compassionate quality and capacity to redress the alleged unfairness of performance-based distribution of rewards. It turned out, however, that too large a dose of equality (to say nothing about the all too visible state hand in managing the economy) gradually began to reduce the yearly increments of wealth created and may even at one point have reached a stage when the absolute amount of wealth created began to decrease. Under the circumstances, the alternatives of either more equality at the cost of a shrinking economic pie and falling living standards, or more performance-based inequality resulting in a growing pie and rising living standards, have become more sharply defined than ever.

In a world of dynamic technology and changing demand no *status quo* can be maintained for long. The resurgent market system with its accompanying greater innovativeness, entrepreneurship and competition, strengthened by the main thrust of technological change, offers encouraging prospects for growth, transformation and well-being. At the same time it is better able to cope with the problems of unemployment and adjustment. The market system is well equipped to solve these problems, or alleviate their effects, for at least two reasons. *First*, it will be doing so under conditions of stronger economic growth than its collectivist and etatist alternative and, *second*, it will have more effective instruments at its disposal. Lowered, simplified, and indexed income taxes, made additionally more just by a drastic reduction in tax exemptions serving special causes and vested interest groups — like that introduced recently in the US — are generally less damaging to incentives to work in the long run. These and other market-reinforcing measures make the economy more flexible and, as such, better able to cope with structural change. Structural change under conditions of higher economic growth is in turn the best recipe for solving the unemployment dilemma.

JOB SATISFACTION

It is also worth realizing that under the resurgent market system alternative jobs will, on average, be more satisfying. Where structural change is resisted rather than encouraged, the proportion of interesting jobs in expanding R- and D-based industries and, to a much larger extent, in information-processing services will definitely be smaller. Thus, the 'new individualism', as this author dubbed the emerging liberal, market-oriented order, is likely to be not only more efficient and, as such, more rewarding in terms of consumption, but also more rewarding in terms of job satisfaction. It is better able to generate not only more innovation and entrepreneurship from the best but also more willingness to make extra effort from the majority. The frequently encountered attitude best expressed in a French expression: "First of all, not too much zeal" would begin to recede.

Even on the left one may find signs of recognition that there is little in terms of income, satisfaction and freedom that the collectivist-etatist alternative would be able to provide over and above what is already provided by or can be expected from capitalism and liberal democracy. Nothing is perhaps more telling than the results of a 1985 French survey showing that even a majority of supporters of the French communist party who had any opinion at all expected the liberal market-oriented order to accelerate growth, reduce unemployment, increase the purchasing power of wages and even reduce inequality (*L'Expansion*, 1985, February 8). And this is the most Stalinist party in Western Europe!

BETTER STANDARD

As some new leftist critics of social-democratic policies point out (see, e.g. Selbourne, 1985), the majority of the working class accepted capitalism long ago. It enjoys both a level of supply and a variety of consumer goods and services far greater than under any alternative, as well as the freedom resulting from democracy, which is unavailable at all elsewhere. Over time it may even recognize what Selbourne does not seem to be able to, namely that if capitalism *cum* democracy are superior to socialism, the latter ceases to be a serious alternative. What is left is socialist *policies* that become only corrections or distortions of the superior liberal, market-oriented alternative.

But what if preferences for the collectivist-etatist utopia remain strong enough to disregard its impact upon both wealth and democracy? The conclusion to be drawn from scenario three is that under such circumstances a decreasingly competitive, structurally obsolete economy is going to generate a 'stop the world I want to get off' syndrome that will result in a further steep fall in living standards through despecialization, possibly coupled with a sharp curtailment of political freedom. And the smaller the country that decided upon such an alternative, the steeper would be the fall. This author does not, however, see too many candidates among Western societies ready to persist in sacrificing both wellbeing *and* freedom in pursuit of an increasingly impoverishing and coercive utopia.

FREEDOM FOR GOOD MEASURE

Finally, let it be noted that the above conclusions were couched in terms of efficiency and satisfaction. Two very important criteria which in themselves would point to the superiority of the capitalist, private enterprise-based market-oriented order were consciously put aside. Those who value political freedom above all would prefer it because freedom has never flourished in any other economic system regardless of relative efficiency. And to those concerned with religious needs the liberal order offers at least a tolerant environment because it is free from the *cuius regio eius religio* temptation of more centralized and activist political and economic orders.

NOTES

1. The exercise has been done in J. Winiecki's 'Economic Trends and Prospects in Comparative Perspective', East, Warsaw, October 1984 (mimeo).

2. Input-output tables deal with product groups rather than with administrative groupings, but administrative groupings in STEs were after all created to manage more or less homogeneous product groups.

3. The term was quoted in *Rabotnichesko delo*, (31 May 1983).

4. In the Soviet parlance 'intensive' economic growth is what STEs have been aiming at in the past quarter of a century, i.e. more efficient use of the already employed factors of production and the substitution of qualitatively better factors for the existing lower quality factors. 'Extensive' economic growth is by the same token growth through additions of (qualitatively the same) production factors.

5. More accurately, further transfers of labour out of agriculture are not possible without fundamental changes in collectivised agriculture.

6. Furthermore, as has often happened in practice, increased productivity resulting from innovation could result only in increased plan targets in the next planning period, so the extra effort would even be counterproductive, for it would be more difficult to implement the next year's plan and earn the associated bonuses.

7. The effects of these advantages were reduced, however, by the lasting tendency to exceed the optimum production scale. Giantomania, in turn, raised costs, disproportionately increased pollution, etc.; thus reducing the gains from large-scale operations.

8. Poland, Czechoslovakia and the Soviet Union are exceptions here, Hungary's record is spotty if the whole decade is taken into consideration, while in Bulgaria there has even been an improvement. The GDR and Romania held constant (although at different levels).

9. It is a good indicator of falling product quality that in Poland and Romania, the two countries that experienced the steepest decline in living standards, there are more official statements and party directives on upgrading product quality than ever. The late general secretary Andropov's utterances about the low quality of Soviet products also caught the attention of the foreign press. Bulgaria, too, held a party plenum devoted to quality in 1984, indicating mounting difficulties in this respect.

10. It is worth noting that even China showed similar high energy consumption per unit of GDP (1.5 kg of coal equivalent per dollar of GDP around 1975), in spite of the fact that its GNP *per capita* level was about 10 times smaller.

11. It is difficult to compare completion periods on a project-type basis because of the more sophisticated technology used now than, say, 20 years ago. However, we may deduce an increasing lag in this respect from the ratio of unfinished investments to annual investment in those countries that publish the respective time series. The ratio for Bulgaria, Czechoslovakia, Hungary and the Soviet Union was on the average markedly higher in the 1970s than in the 1960s, with the tendency to increase towards the end of the 1970s.

12. NMP is equal to GNP *less* services regarded as 'non-material' and *less* depreciation.

13. Transport intensity is very much higher in the Soviet Union (the separate curve for the Soviet Union is not shown in Figure 2).

14. The data were taken from a Czechoslovak source, *Zahranicni obchod*, (1983).

15. Some figures were overstated in a worse way during the Stalinist period but then high economic growth spurred by forced industrialisation was regarded by communist elites as a *quid pro quo*. No such *quid pro quo* can be identified now.

16. Changes in the way the consumer prices index (CPI) is constructed took place in Poland in two stages: in the mid-1970s and in 1981. At present the CPI in Poland does not differ much with respect to its construction method from that in Hungary (and generally in MEs).

17. E.g. a general rise in food prices in Bulgaria in 1968 ranging from 30% to 100% on most products was officially registered as a 4-5% increase in the CPI. Given the high share of food in total consumer expenditures (above 50% at the time), this CPI increase was grossly understated. Also, more recently, in Czechoslovakia the CPI increase for the 1982-83 period was officially put at 7%. But at the same time prices of beef increased by 60%, veal by 42%, pork by 35%, ham and sausages by 20%, fish by 30-55%, prices of consumer durables like colour TV sets increased by 40%, automatic washing machines by 24%, electric cookers by 23%, the price of petrol by 23%, and so on.

18. The results and the methodology are presented in *Economic Bulletin for Europe*, 31, No. 2 (1980). The methodology is, in short, based upon selected physical flow and stock indicators that correlate most highly with GDP *per capita* levels in benchmark years over the whole period under consideration. The regression equations thus obtained were then used to predict GDP *per capita* for a given country in a given benchmark year on the basis of the arithmetic average of all the GDP *per capita* levels predicted for each country from all 25-30 equations. Growth rates of GDP *per capita* were then calculated between benchmark years.

19. Interestingly, although not entirely convincingly, Alton's estimates for Hungary show growth overstatements for that country being about average relative to those of other STEs in question for the 1975-1982 period and being worst of all countries for the 1970-1975 period. Various estimates of living standards and GNP *per capita* show a smaller difference between, say, Czechoslovakia and GDR on the one hand and Hungary on the other than could be expected on the basis of official figures. Marer's (1985) estimates showed a smaller difference between Hungary and these countries. Since it is commonly assumed that the reduction of this difference took place in the 1970s rather than earlier, there is a strong probability that it is the statistics of other countries showing higher growth rates than the Hungarian ones that are more badly overstated.

20. It is steady encouragement of entrepreneurship rather than the actual numbers that matters in the long term; for in Poland small private businesses expanded somewhat faster in the early 1980s, but are now either shrinking or reorienting themselves towards a short-term profit maximisation strategy in an increasingly hostile environment.

21. According to *Zycie gospodarcze*, 1984, No. 40, only about half of consumer durables was sold through normal distribution channels in the Krakow region, while about 45% was rationed 'on a personal basis'. The data exclude cars, but the situation in the car market is not greatly different, according to other sources. There is no reason to assume that the Krakow region is in any way different from the rest of Poland.

22. However, although there is no conflict of economic interest, there may be problems of psychological adaptation to a decentralised, market-based economic system, for both the military and the police are hierarchical, multi-level organisations and central planning may seem more 'natural' to people coming from such organisations.

23. In the Sudan the regime change towards greater reliance on the market occurred without personal change at the top.

24. A 1982 poll showed that the public in the five largest West European countries overestimated enterprises after-tax profits on fairly standardized consumer goods on average by a factor of ten (*Financial Times*, 1982, July 5).

25. The disincentives affect effort rather than the higher education itself since the latter may be highly valued, given the family tradition of the large part of would-be students.

26. The understanding seems to be on the increase, though. See, e.g. Saxonhouse (1983).

27. Constraints stemming from the impact of redistributive coalitions, trade unions, should be included under the same heading.

28. Their bargaining position *vis-à-vis* interventionist governments would also be strengthened by employment implications of their failures.

29. This author accepts the Aristotelian distinction between numerical equality which the author calls egalitarianism, proportional equality, based on performance as the criterion of distribution, which he calls justice, and equity, i.e. correction of distribution according to performance on the basis of some other criteria (compassion, solidarity, etc.).

30. Interestingly, Shonfield, born in Poland, decided not to go back after the communist takeover, admitting implicitly that the totalitarian version of collectivism meant *too much* government intervention ...

31. Many intellectuals not belonging to the far left miss the point even now; see, e.g. the results of a survey of American newspaper reporters. The survey as reported in Evans (1984) revealed strong negative correlation between the disagreement with the statement: "Political democracy is impossible in absence of free enterprise" and adoption by journalists of a socialdemocratic ("liberal" in American parlance) ideological outlook. Incidentally, journalists hold this outlook almost 2.5 times as often as the general public. The American press tends to be much more critical of the capitalist, private enterprise-oriented market system and much more interventionist than other professional groups in the United States.

32. Taking Sweden as an example: firm-specific subsidies for shipyards in 1977-1979 were equal to 120.2% of the total wage bill in the shipbuilding industry; subsidies for steel making and mining were equal to 33.4% and 40% of the total wage bills respectively *(IUI Yearbook 1982-1983)*.

33. Doubts concern the fact that *European Management Forum's Report on International Competitiveness* (1985) puts West Germany near the top of the league of industrial competitiveness, the criteria for which include also microeconomic flexibility. Austria is not very far behind either (11th in 1985, 7th in 1984).

34. See, e.g. the report by the Netherlands Scientific Council for Government Policy (1985).

35. A concept more appealing to this author, because more in tune with the 'new indivisualism' of a liberal market-oriented order, would be the one proposed by Samuel Brittan (*Financial Times*, 1983, November 17), i.e. 'people's capitalism' through distribution of shares among all citizens.

36. In Yugoslavia the superiority of the market economy may not have been so evident and illusions with respect to the expected performance of self-management economy much stronger than in Poland some thirty years later.

37. This is, these authors stress, the essence of theory of the dualism of human needs by the psychologist Ernest Becker.

38. The renunciation of the myth of an intrinsic value of the labour-managed firm would entail a rejection of the idea of uniformity of workers' needs. For some employees working environment would be the place chosen for fulfilling the need to excel (in better managed business organizations the share of such employees would certainly be larger), for others the community would be this place and for yet another, smaller group only the national level would suffice (their needs would be satisfied by participation in national politics). Finally, some would not feel such needs at all. Recognition of this diversity does, however, not come easily to those wanting to make everybody happy by applying uniform measures from above.

39. The term used, amongst others, by Jacques Juillard, a columnist of the leftist French weekly *Le Nouvel Observateur*, which now regards as its vocation to accommodate French left-leaning parties with enterprise, profits and markets to free the left from this fixation.

40. Hager (1982) also notices this phenomenon, although he does not pinpoint its peculiarities.

41. Such measures would not be based on justice or equality. Such or similar measures were not introduced when workers (and owners) in other industries had to adapt to change in demand and competitiveness. Their rationale should be based mainly on efficiency: logic demands measures making resistance to necessary change less disruptive and costly.

42. It would be interesting to see the results of a cross-national study comparing voting patterns of private and public sector employees.

43. Burenstam-Linder (1985) advance this argument with respect to the impact of market-based successes of the Pacific Basin countries.

44. Interestingly, the Yugoslav practice combined a high level of investment with its low efficiency, implying simultaneously overinvestment and unemployment.

REFERENCES

Alton, T.P., 1985, East European GNPs: Origins of Product, Final Uses, Rates of Growth, and International Comparisons, in: *East European Economies: Slow Growth in the 1980s*, Vol.1, J.E.C., U.S. Congress, Washington D.C.

Askanas, B., and K. Laski, 1985, Consumer Prices and Private Consumption in Poland and Austria, *Journal of Comparative Economics*, Vol.9, No.2.

Baechler, J., 1980, Liberty, Property, and Equality, *Nomos*, Vol.2.

Balassa, B., 1984, The Economic Consequences of Social Policies in the Industrial Countries, *Weltwirtschaftliches Archiv*, Bd.120, Heft 2.

Bauer, T., 1984, The Second Economic Reform and Ownership Relations, *East European Economics*.

Berliner, J.S., 1976, *The Innovation Decision in Soviet Industry*, MIT Press, Cambridge, Mass.

Birch, D.L., 1981, Who Creates Jobs?, *Public Interest*, No.65, Fall.

Blackhurst, R., 1981, The Twilight of Domestic Economic Policies, *World Economy*, No.4.

Bognar, J., 1982, *Balance of Achievements of Twenty-Five Years of Hungary's Economic Development*, Hungarian Scientific Council for World Economy, Budapest.

Buchanan, J.M., 1979, Politics Without Romance: A Sketch of Positive Public Choice Theory and Its Normative Implications, *IHS Journal*, No.3/ reprinted in: *The Theory of Public Choice-II*, The University of Michigan Press, Ann Arbor, 1984.

Burenstam-Linder, S., 1985, Pacific Protagonist — Implications of the Rising Role of the Pacific, *American Economic Review*, Vol.75, No.2.

Carlsson, B., 1980, *The Swedish Economy Facing the 80s*. Booklet from IUI No.108, Stockholm.

CEPII, 1983, *Economie mondiale: la montee des tensions*. Rapport du ..., Economica, Paris.

Chapman, J.W., 1980, Justice, Freedom and Property, *Nomos*, Vol.22.

Closet, F. de, 1982, *Toujours plus*, Paris.

Csaba, L., 1983, New Features of the Hungarian Economic Mechanism in the Mid-Eighties, *New Hungarian Quarterly*, Vol.24, No.90, Summer.

Csikos-Nagy, B., 1975, *Socialist Price Theory and Price Policy*, Akademiai Kiado, Budapest.

Csikos-Nagy, B., and L. Racz, 1983, Rise of the Price Level and Its Factors in Hungary, *Acta Oeconomica*, Vol.30, No.2.

Deutsch, K., 1966, *The Nerves of Government*, Models of Political Communication and Control, The Free Press, New York.

Drewnowski, J., 1982, The Anatomy of Economic Failure in Soviet-type Systems, in: *Crisis in the East European Economies*, Ed. by J. Drewnowski, Croom Helm, London.

Economic Survey of Europe, 1969, 1982.

Economic Bulletin for Europe, 1980, Vol.31, No.2.

Eliasson, G., 1985, *The Stability of Economic Organizational Forms and the Importance of Human Capital*, The Industrial Institute for Economic and Social Research, Working Paper No.143, Stockholm (mimeo).

European Management Forum, 1985, *EMF's Report on International Competitiveness*, Cologny/Geneva.

Evans, F. J., 1984, The Politics of the Press, *Business Horizons*, Vol.27, No.2.

Fein, T. S., 1980, Self-Employed Americans: Their Number has Increased, *Monthly Labor Review*, November, No.11.

Fitzroy, F. R., 1981, Work-Sharing and Insurance Policy: A Cure for Stagflation, *Kyklos*, Vol.34, Fasc.3.

Gomulka, S., 1982, The Polish Crisis: Will It Spread and What Will Be The Outcome? in: *Crisis in the East European Economy*, Ed. by J. Drewnowski, Croom Helm, London.

Hager, E., 1982, Industrial Policy, Trade Policy, and European Social Democracy, in: *National Industrial Strategies and the World Economy*. Ed. by J. Pinder, Croom Helm, London.

Hawrylyshyn, B., 1980, *Road Maps to the Future. Towards More Effective Societies*. A Report to the Club of Rome, Pergamon Press, Oxford.

Holzman, F.D., 1979, Some Systemic Factors Contributing to the Convertible Currency Shortages of Centrally Planned Economies, *American Economic Review*, Vol.69, No.2.

Ingelstam, L., 1983, A Third Sector Approach to Sweden's Future, *Futures*, Vol.15, No.2, April.

Interfutures, *Facing the Future*, OECD, 1979.

IUI Yearbook, 1982-1983, *Microeconometrics*, Stockholm, 1983.

J.E.C., 1982, USSR: *Measures of Economic Growth and Development, 1950-1980*. A study prepared for the use of Joint Economic Committee, U.S. Congress, Washington D.C.

Kaldor, N., 1934, The Equilibrium of the Firm, *Economic Journal*, Vol.44, March, No.173.

Kemenes, E., 1979, L'economie hongroise dans les relations Est-Ouest, in: *Regulation et division internationale du travail*, F. Renversez and M. Lavigne (eds.), Economica, Paris.

Kimball, T.L., 1973, I Felt the Winds of Change in Russia, *National Wildlife*, February-March.

Kindleberger, C.P., 1978, The Ageing Economy, *Weltwirtschaftliches Archiv*, Band 114, Heft 3.

Kornai J., 1979, Resource-Constrained versus Demand-Constrained Systems, *Econometrica*, Vol.47, No.4.

Kornai, J., 1980, *The Economics of Shortage*, Amsterdam, North Holland.

Kornai, J., 1984, Bureaucratic and Market Coordination, *Osteuropa Wirtschaft*, Vol.29, Heft 4.

Kristensen, O.P., 1982, Voter Attitudes and Public Spending: Is There a Relationship? *European Journal of Political Research*, Vol.10.

Laski, K., 1977, *Inflationsprobleme in den sozialistischen Landern*, Wien Institut fur Internationale Wirtschaftsvergleiche, Forschungsberichte No.38.

Lawrance, R.Z., 1983, The Myth of U.S. Deindustrialization, *Challenge*, Vol.26, November-December, No.5.

Leroux, A., 1986, A chacun son totem, *L'Expansion*, 18 juillet/11 septembre.

Lindbeck, A., 1981a, *The Distribution of Factor Income versus Disposable Income in a Welfare State*. The Case of Sweden. Seminar Paper No.171. Institute for International Economic Studies, Stockholm (mimeo).

Lindbeck, A., 1981b, *Work Disincentives in the Welfare State*, Reprint Series No.176, Institute for International Economic Studies, Stockholm.

Lindbeck, A., 1982, *Emerging Arteriosclerosis of the Western Economies*. Institute for International Economic Studies, Reprint Series No.191, Stockholm.

Lundberg, E., 1983, Options of Small Economies During the Crisis, in: *Strukturpolitik als Dimension der Vollbeschaftigungspolitik*. Ed. by H. Kramer and F. Butschek, Fischer Verlag, Vienna.

Marer, P., 1985, Alternative Estimates of the Dollar GNP and Growth Rates of the CMEA Countries, in: *East European Economies: Slow Growth in the 1980s*, Vol.1, J.E.C., U.S. Congress, Washington D.C.

Mosoczy, R., 1983, Possibilities and Trends in the Development of International Cooperation in the 1980s, *Acta Oeconomica*, Vol.30, Nos.3-4.

Netherlands Scientific Council for Government Policy, 1985, *Safeguarding Social Security*, The Hague.

North, D.C., and R.P. Thomas, 1973, *The Rise of the West: A New Economic History*, Cambridge University Press, Cambridge.

Nove, A., 1977, *The Soviet Economic System*, London.

Oates, W.C., Markets for Pollution Control, *Challenge*, Vol.27, May/June, No.2.

O'Dowd, M.C., 1980, There is Nothing New under the Sun, *World Economy*, Vol.3, September, No.2.

Olson, M., 1982, *The Rise and Decline of Nations*, Yale University Press, New Haven.

Peters, T.J., and R.H. Waterman, Jr, 1982, *In Search of Excellence*, Harper and Row, New York.

Pindak, F., 1983, Inflation under Central Planning, *Jahrbuch der Wirtschaft Osteuropas*, Vol.II.

Pinder, J., 1982, Industrial Policy and the International Economy in: *National Strategies and the World Economy*. Ed. by J. Pinder, Allanheld Osmun, Totowa, N.J.

Pitt, D., and S. Booth, 1983, Paradigms Lost? Reflections on the coming organizational "revolution", *Futures*, Vol.15, June, No.3.

Postel, S., 1984, *Air Pollution, Acid Rain, and the Future of Forests*, World-watch Paper 58, Washington D.C.

Poznanski, K., 1986, Competition Between Eastern Europe and Developing Countries in the Western Market for Manufactured Goods, *East European Economies: Slow Growth in the 1980s*, Vol.3, J.E.C., U.S. Congress, Washington D.C.

Report of European Trade Union Institute, 1979, *Keynes Plus a Participatory Economy*, Brussels.

Robinson, J., 1934, Euler's Theorem and the Problem of Distribution, *Economic Journal*, No.44, September, No.175.

Saxonhouse, G.R., 1983, What Is All This About "Industrial Targeting" in Japan, *World Economy*, Vol.6, September, No.3.

Schultz, G.P., 1981, The Comparative Advantage of Government: A Commentary, *Economic Impact*, No.36.

Selbourne, D., 1985, *Against Socialist Illusion: A Radical Argument*, Macmillan, London.

Servan-Schreiber, J.J., 1968, *Le Defi Americain*, Denoel, Paris.

Shonfield, A., 1965, *Modern Capitalism. The Changing Balance of Public and Private Power*, Oxford University Press, London.

Smil, V., and T. Kuz, 1976, A new look at energy and GNP correlations, *Energy International*, January.

Wildavsky, A., 1980, *How to Limit Government Spending*, Berkeley, University of California Press.

Wiles, P.J.D., 1977, *Economic Institutions Compared*, Basil Blackwell, Oxford.

Wiles, P.J.D., 1982, Zero Growth and the International Nature of the Polish Disease, in: *Crisis in the East European Economies*, Ed. by J. Drewnowski, Croom Helm, London.

Wiles, P.J.D., 1983, Soviet Inflation, 1982, *Jahrbuch der Wirtschaft Osteuropas*, Vol.II.

Winiecki, J., 1978, Sources of Inflation in the Western Economies. Some Theoretical Considerations, *Maandschrift Economie*, No.11/12.

Winiecki, J., 1980, *Mecanisme: productivite — profits — salaires — couts — prix — en tant que source de l'inflation dans l'economic de marche.* Prepare pour la Conferance franco-polonaise "Inflation et cycle conjonctural dans les pays capitalistes industrialises", Varsovie, 17-19 september 1980 (mimeo).

Winiecki, J., 1982, Investment Cycles and an Excess Demand Inflation in Planned Economies: Sources and Processes, *Acta Oeconomica*, Vol.28, No.1-2.

Winiecki, J., 1983, Resource Constraints and Eastern Foreign Trade Structures, *Intereconomics*, No.3.

Winiecki, J., 1984a, *Economic Trends and Prospects in Comparative Perspective: East*, mimeo (original essay).

Winiecki, J., 1984b, *The Overgrown Industrial Sector in Soviet-Type Economies: Explanations, Evidence, Consequences,* Warsaw, mimeo.

Winiecki, J., 1985a, Planification centrale et exportation des produits manufactures (considerations theorique sur l'impact du systeme centralement planifie sur la specialisation), *Revue d'etudes comparatives Est-Ouest,* Vol.16, No.2.

Winiecki, J., 1985b, Inflation under Central Planning: Sources, Processes and Manifestations, *Konjunkturpolitik,* Heft 4/5.

Winiecki, J., 1986a, Distorted Macroeconomics of Central Planning, *Banca Nazionale del Lavoro,* No.157.

Winiecki, J., 1986b, The Overgrown Industrial Sector in Soviet-Type Economies: Explanations, Evidence, Consequences, *Comparative Economic Studies* (forthcoming).

Winiecki, J., 1986c, Inflation Under Market and Plan, PWN Publishers, Warsaw, (in Polish).

Winiecki, J., 1986d, *Why Economic Reforms Fail in the Soviet System? A Property Rights - Based Approach,* Warsaw (mimeo).

A Comment on
Technology, Restructuring,
People's Reaction and Reform

Roger Clarke

Biographical note

Roger Clarke was born in 1940 and educated at Gresham's School, Holt, and Glasgow University, where he studied modern languages and economics. From 1965 he has worked at the Institute of Soviet and East European Studies in Glasgow, being deputy editor of *Soviet Studies* in 1973-1978 and Editor since 1978.

His publications include *Soviet Economic Facts 1917-1971* (updated and expanded edition *Soviet Economic Facts 1917-1981* with D. J. I. Matko), *Comecon, Trade and the West* (with William V. Wallace) and a variety of articles on Soviet and East European affairs, mostly published in *Soviet Studies*. He has also translated several works in the field from German and Polish.

His major current interest is economic reform in Soviet-type economies, especially Poland and Hungary.

May I start by saying how pleased and honoured I felt when Ljubo Sirc invited me to contribute a comment on this work by Jan Winiecki. Winiecki was known to me and had impressed me as the author of the two articles I published in *Soviet Studies* in July and October 1986, and subsequently, in Warsaw, I enjoyed an evening of most interesting conversation with him on a wide range of economic, social and political affairs. Even so, I found the clarity and the breadth of this work, and the variety of sources on which the author draws, highly impressive.

East knows West

Some readers may be a little surprised to find an economist from Poland as the author of a work of which the larger part deals with Western economies. To this I would make two points. First, it should be no more surprising that a Polish economist studies and writes about the economies of the West than that British or American economists study and write about the economies of the East. The fact that this has been unusual is a reflection of the nature of the Eastern societies. I view Winiecki's work as an example of what I see as the encouraging and desirable trend for at least some East European countries, mainly Poland and Hungary so far, to be re-integrated into European and world intellectual life after the postwar period of isolation. Second, I submit that we in the West should pay particular attention when a professional economist who also has personal experiences of life in an economy not based on private enterprise and the market warns us of the debilitating effects of abandoning these principles.

1. DIRECTION OF TECHNOLOGICAL CHANGE

After this preamble, I want to comment briefly on two specific points in Winiecki's work. I shall then go on to discuss two other issues arising from it at slightly greater length. First, on the subject of the direction of technological change. I agree wholeheartedly with and would like to emphasise the importance Winiecki attaches to the switch away from change based on increasing economies of scale. The technological requirement for large numbers of people to work together in one establishment was a characteristic of industrial society which distinguished it from pre-industrial society, and had wide-ranging consequences on attitudes, and on settlement patterns — it led to the creation of large industrial towns. Two to three decades ago, I think, this began to alter, with increasing automation of physical operations and simultaneous improvement and cheapening of communications. To the economic, social and political consequences which Winiecki discusses I would add one question. What are the implications of this technological trend for the much-discussed 'problem of the inner cities'? I am not sure that sufficient thought has been given to this in the context of policies to deal with the problem. Do people actually want to go on living in such large urban agglomerations now that it is less technologically necessary? In Britain at least there seems to me to be a lot of evidence that many do not.

The question I have just raised about cities may be regarded as something of an aside in the present context. The other comment I want to make about the direction technological change has assumed is absolutely central to the future of Soviet-type economies. While it is implicit in what he says, I feel that Winiecki could with advantage make more of the consequences of this new direction for the STEs. The high level of complex, two-way interdependence between a large number of comparatively small (quite often very small) firms which is characteristic of many of the new electronics-based industries is above all the kind of industrial structure with which the central planning system cannot cope. I think this adds an additional dimension to the argument, made by Winiecki and many others, that as the Soviet-type economies have developed and become more complex their system has become increasingly clumsy and inappropriate. The fact that further development now requires a growing proportion of sectors in the economy which need a structure of precisely the type least compatible with centralised planning and administration powerfully reinforces all that Winiecki says about systemic resistance to innovation, and I think it is worth emphasising this specifically.

2. THINGS GETTING BAD ENOUGH

The second subject on which I want to comment is the reaction to a deteriorating economic situation. When writing about the West, Winiecki quotes George Schultz: 'When things get bad enough people do even obvious and sensible things.' By the end of the 1970s several Western societies did indeed react in a way which seems to confirm this dictum — for which we may feel profoundly grateful and encouraged. And it is consistent with this observation that Winiecki attaches quite a low probability to his pessimistic scenario for the West, and higher probabilities to his optimistic and semi-optimistic ones. Yet when he writes about the East, he attaches only a low possibility of fulfilment to his only semi-optimistic scenario. I am certainly not contesting his judgement of the probabilities, in East or West, but I do find myself wondering if we are being inconsistent. At what point will things in the East be bad enough to cause people to do obvious and sensible things?

They are already much worse than they were in the West in the late 1970s, surely! Of course, the lack of political democracy in the East is a large part of the explanation, but I think that a more fundamental issue is also raised here. The argument that sooner or later economic deterioration will lead to serious (and by implication successful) economic reform in Eastern Europe is a common one. Yet it seems to me to ignore the fact that, historically, different areas of the world have indeed risen and fallen economically relative to one another. Does this not show that decline may evoke only unsuccessful attempts to stop it, or no attempt at all? I suggest two conclusions. First, we in the West should not be complacent: we may have come to our senses in time, but the danger is not permanently banished — long-term decline *is* possible. Second, for the East, fundamental political change in the direction of democracy may be an essential pre-condition for substantial and lasting economic recovery, allowing people — meaning the mass of society — to choose governments that will do the obvious and sensible things.

3. RESTRUCTURING THE ECONOMY

Following these direct comments on particular points in Winiecki's work, I would now like to say a little more about two topics which are central to discussion of the future of the East European economies. These are, first, restructuring of the economy and, second reform of the economic system. They are conceptually distinct, but in practice turn out to be closely interrelated.

In the debate about the comparative merits of central planning and the market, one of the leading arguments for central planning used to be its claimed ability to implement a co-ordinated structural policy based on a national view of the economy's requirements, undistorted by considerations of the individual firm's profits. There is a simple and appealing logic in this argument. But in practice it turns out to be completely wrong. Changing the structure of Soviet-type economies has been found to be extremely hard, once the system and pattern of industrialisation have been established. (I am not questioning the fact that the system created basic heavy industries quickly in a mainly agricultural economy.) This is true both of the traditional type of central planning, and of the Hungarian 'reformed' system. In the former, the method by which the planning is, and can only be, done, 'planning from the achieved level', is one major reason. Output plans are decided by adjusting those of the previous year — and there is a strongly entrenched presumption that all such adjustments will be upward ones. This approach tends to preserve the existing structure. The second reason change is so difficult is the political clout of representatives of the established industries in a decision-making process which is essentially political rather than economic. The situation is far more conducive to lobbying, and the economic costs and benefits far harder to identify, than in market economies (where lobbying for political support of economically declining industries is also of course entirely familiar).

In the Hungarian system restructuring is a major problem, too, and here its connection with reform of the system is particularly clear. Although the Hungarian central authorities do not set enterprise plans, and enterprises are supposed to be profitable, the scope for bargaining between managers of large enterprises and the central authorities over taxes, credits and even direct subsidies, and again the political nature of the process, make it very hard in practice to enforce the rundown of unprofitable but well established and powerful industries. The phenomenon will be easily recognised by British readers who remember the 1970s. Full and consistent implementation of the reformers' market principles, with bankruptcy for chronically unprofitable enterprises, and enforcement of universal rather than individual tax and credit policies, would force restructuring to more profitable industries. Therefore the old-established industries are a major centre of resistance to further reform (or rather to full implementation of the reforms already announced). The general lesson, transcending different systems, seems to me to be that government, and political processes, must be separated from the making of decisions about economic matters as far as possible. State ownership is thus a severe disadvantage, because government is then by definition involved. Private ownership, whilst inherently preferable, however, must not be weakened by the creation of a political climate in which government is expected to be able to solve all difficulties.

De-Industrialisation?

It is worth drawing attention at this juncture to what Winiecki shows us about the excessive development of industry in the East, and his remarks on 'industrial romanticism' in the West. These should be commended especially to those who now criticise what they call 'de-industrialisation', which I see more as a process of catching up on the restructuring delayed in the 1970s and earlier. I would like to quote a number of Hungarian economists with whom I discussed the restructuring question: when I asked if they had any proposals for industries which should be developed to replace the metallurgical and chemical sectors, which have become widely unprofitable there, the reply was simply 'profitable ones'; it was for enterprise managements to find out what activities were profitable in a market system. The contrast with the notion of governments 'picking winners' is striking.

4. IMPROVED UNDERSTANDING OF REFORM

Finally, a few words on reforming Soviet-type economies. I

am not entirely happy about Winiecki's analogy of re-inventing the wheel, because I see the market as more akin to a naturally occurring phenomenon than an invention. It is known that societies have existed which have been ignorant of the wheel. They could then have invented it for themselves, or learnt of its existence elsewhere and imported it, or, of course, continued in ignorance of it. Except in the sense of the organised market place, the rudiments of market relations, exchange of goods or services, have surely always existed, though of course the extent to which they have been developed varied widely. The Soviet-type economies do not have to re-invent the market — most of their citizens are well aware of its existence, and in some of them there are many able economists, like Winiecki, who have a high level of understanding of how it works. So it is not a matter of re-invention, but of will to abolish the restrictions which prevent the market from working.

Economic reform is an area in which I do think that scholars in West and East can justly claim that their understanding has advanced considerably over the past ten decades. During the first wave of reforms in the STEs in the middle and late 1960s it seemed to be generally thought that almost any piecemeal steps in the direction of decentralisation were helpful. By the late 1970s it was widely recognised that, to have any chance of success, reform must be a comprehensive and consistent package; otherwise the traditional central planning system swamped the reform and reasserted itself. Until comparatively recently, most discussion of reform has implicitly assumed that the difficult part about serious reform was getting the top-level decision to introduce it. Whilst this clearly remains a major difficulty, and Winiecki has an interesting and illuminating discussion of the reasons, I think it is only now becoming apparent how difficult the process of reforming a Soviet-type economy is, even given a top-level decision.

My basis for saying this is mainly Hungarian experience. I think it can be accepted that the Hungarian leadership did intend the New Economic Mechanism introduced in 1968 to be a major change in the economic system (though not, of course, a full return to a private-enterprise market economy). Yet after nearly twenty years the extent of specifically systemic change is quite limited. Many of the ways in which life in Hungary is easier than in other East European countries are due to other policy changes (greater freedom for travel, less politicisation of life) or to toleration of the growth of a 'second', more consumer-oriented economy around the 'first' economy (private agriculture, trade, services are much less restricted). The more one discusses the large scale state sector of the Hungarian economy with Hungarian economists, the less it seems to differ from the other STEs. We have already referred to tax and credit bargaining and the way they undermine the market discipline. More fundamentally, the meaning of economic concepts, above all of profits, in these conditions is highly questionable. In essence, the role of political elements in economic decisions is still far too large, and it seems to me more and more that political reform, particularly the reduction of the role of government and, crucially, of the Communist party, in the operation of the economy is an essential precondition for successful reform. And in the light of Winiecki's discussion of how these people benefit from their role in the economy it must be doubtful if this is possible without ending Communist rule. Economic reform, I find myself concluding, has only limited prospects of success without fundamental political change, and is a far more difficult process than has generally been imagined.

For Product Safety Concerns and Information please contact our EU
representative GPSR@taylorandfrancis.com Taylor & Francis Verlag GmbH,
Kaufingerstraße 24, 80331 München, Germany

Printed and bound by CPI Group (UK) Ltd, Croydon, CR0 4YY
01/05/2025
01858459-0001